SERVING
Gifted Students
WITHIN AN
RtI Framework

A Practical Guide

D1166236

SERVING
Gifted Students
WITHIN AN
RtI Framework
A Practical Guide

SUSAN K. JOHNSEN, PH.D.,
TRACEY N. SULAK, & KAREN ROLLINS

PRUFROCK PRESS INC.
WACO, TEXAS

Library of Congress Cataloging-in-Publication Data

Johnsen, Susan K.
 Serving gifted students within an RTI framework / by Susan K. Johnsen, Tracey N. Sulak, and
Karen Rollins.
    p. cm.
Includes bibliographical references.
ISBN 978-1-59363-889-4 (pbk.)
1. Gifted children--Education--United States. 2. Response to intervention (Learning disabled
children)--United States. I. Sulak, Tracey N., 1975- II. Rollins, Karen, 1961- III. Title.
LC3993.9.J62 2012
371.950973--dc23
                                2011050420

Edited by Jennifer Robins

Cover and layout design by Raquel Trevino

ISBN-13: 978-1-59363-889-4

Printed in the United States of America.

At the time of this book's publication, all facts and figures cited are the most current available.
All telephone numbers, addresses, and website URLs are accurate and active. All publications,
organizations, websites, and other resources exist as described in the book, and all have been
verified. The authors and Prufrock Press Inc. make no warranty or guarantee concerning the
information and materials given out by organizations or content found at websites, and we are
not responsible for any changes that occur after this book's publication. If you find an error,
please contact Prufrock Press Inc.

Prufrock Press Inc.
P.O. Box 8813
Waco, TX 76714-8813
Phone: (800) 998-2208
Fax: (800) 240-0333
http://www.prufrock.com

TABLE OF CONTENTS

124537

Preface

. . . .

Response to Intervention (RtI) was introduced as a part of the Individuals with Disabilities Education Improvement Act of 2004 (IDEA, 2004). As a part of the regulations, each state needed to identify students with learning disabilities using an RtI process. Because specific details were not described, each state and local school district was given the freedom to develop its own RtI procedures. RtI is a process that integrates curriculum and instruction with assessment and a multi-tiered system of increasingly intensive interventions (E. Johnson, Mellard, Fuchs, & McKnight, 2006). Although the process has focused primarily on students who exhibit deficit skills, researchers and policy makers have begun to examine ways that gifted students, particularly those with disabilities, might also be included (Coleman & Johnsen, 2011; Council for Exceptional Children, The Association for the Gifted [CEC-TAG], 2009).

CEC-TAG (2009) developed a position statement addressing the needs of students with gifts and talents and twice-exceptional students (i.e., gifted students with disabilities; see Appendix A). CEC-TAG views

RtI as a schoolwide initiative; because of this, there is a need to involve gifted students within the RtI framework. Therefore, CEC-TAG identified ways that gifted students might be included in universal screening, assessments, and progress monitoring; in established protocols for students needing additional support; in problem-solving approaches tailored to individual students; and in a tiered system of intervention. For this inclusion to occur, the system needs to be flexible and provide appropriate levels of professional development and resources.

Addressing the issues raised in CEC-TAG's position paper, this book, *Serving Gifted Students Within an RtI Framework*, focuses on the key components of RtI: (a) a strong general education curriculum, (b) research-based interventions within a multi-tier system prior to formal identification, (c) assessments that include universal screening and progress monitoring, (d) collaborative problem solving that allows for greater involvement of parents and professionals, and (e) the use of professional development.

Chapter 1 provides an overview of the Response to Intervention process from a special education perspective. This overview includes definitions, approaches to implementing RtI, descriptions and related research evidence for each of the key components, and implementation challenges. Following this introduction, each of the book's chapters addresses ways of incorporating students with gifts and talents within the key component areas.

The first key component, a strong general education curriculum, is addressed in Chapter 2. This chapter begins by describing the national standards in gifted education related to curriculum planning and instruction. Research-based models in gifted education are then presented. These consist of tiered models, curriculum models, models that focus on process development, and domain-specific practices.

Next, Chapter 3 describes tiers of intervention that include students with gifts and talents. For each tier, the chapter discusses curriculum and services for gifted students for each instructional setting, the person responsible for services, assessments of learning, and the duration and goals used to determine placement.

Chapter 4 focuses on assessment. It identifies three categories of formative assessments that are frequently used in the RtI process: universal screening, progress monitoring, and diagnostic assessments. Universal screening is used to identify learners who may need additional interventions and assessments. Progress monitoring includes curriculum-based measurements, classroom assessments, and large-scale assessments. Diagnostic assessments incorporate teacher-made diagnostic tests, achievement tests, and aptitude tests. This chapter describes the psychometric properties and ways of including gifted and talented students in each of type of assessment (including off-level assessments), the use of alternative assessments, and how to determine accelerated progress.

Chapter 5 examines collaboration within the RtI process. The chapter identifies an extensive list of stakeholders who need to be involved at multiple levels. It also examines when and how to use collaboration, as well as the future of the collaboration process. In addition to face-to-face meetings, specific practical strategies are described. Chapter 5 offers a specific collaboration model between universities and schools and stresses the need for including collaboration within professional development and preservice programs. The chapter concludes by emphasizing how successful teamwork and collaboration can assist in all students' success, including students with gifts and talents.

The final chapter considers the needs for professional development. It begins by examining the knowledge and skills necessary for implementing a successful RtI process. Following this introduction, the chapter identifies five roles for all educators (i.e., data-driven decision maker, implementer of evidence-based interventions, provider of differentiated instruction, implementer of socioemotional and behavioral supports, and collaborator) and explains distinct responsibilities for the gifted educator within each role. It concludes by describing the characteristics of successful professional development and how to get started.

Appendix A shares CEC-TAG's position paper on RtI for gifted students, Appendix B highlights online resources to help in implementing RtI, and Appendix C lists state RtI models that include gifted and talented students. We hope that this book is helpful in developing a more inclusive and comprehensive RtI program in your school so that all students will be successful.

CHAPTER

1

Overview of the Response to Intervention Process

. . . .

R esponse to Intervention (RtI) was introduced through the field of special education as part of IDEA 2004 and its consequent regulations. The law stated, "In determining whether a child has a specific learning disability, a local educational agency may use a process that determines if [he or she] responds to scientific, research-based intervention as part of the evaluation process" (20 U.S.C. § 1414[b][6]). The 2006 regulations (§ 300.30[a]) required each state to choose its criteria for identifying students with learning disabilities from among three options: severe discrepancy (may prohibit or permit), RtI (must permit), and other alternative research-based procedures (may permit; Zirkel & Krohn, 2008). Although state agencies "must permit" RtI, specific details were not described within the regulations, which therefore allows states and local schools the freedom to develop their RtI process.

The inclusion of these alternative identification processes within IDEA 2004 was in response to an increase of more than 200% of students identified as having a learning disability since the category was first established in 1977 and concerns about the misidentification of students with learning disabilities using discrepancy formulas (i.e., the difference between performance on intelligence tests and achievement tests; Vaughn, Linan-Thompson, & Hickman, 2003). The notion of discrepancy was initially introduced by Monroe (1932) and represented an operational definition of underachievement. In other words, if a student's performance is in the above average or superior ranges on an intelligence test, indicating potential, and he or she is not achieving in the classroom (e.g., performing 2 years below grade level), then that student is identified as an underachiever. If the discrepancy is determined to be severe, then the student is referred for further testing to determine eligibility for special education services. This determination of severity varies among the states, with some examining standard score differences between test scores (e.g., 20 points) and others using more sophisticated regression formulas (e.g., Wisconsin).

Over the past 20 years, discrepancy formulas have been viewed as not providing sufficient information for interventions, as unreliable and not psychometrically sound, and as preventing students from receiving help until a discrepancy is apparent, which is often at the third grade or later (Fletcher et al., 1998; Vellutino, Scanlon, & Lyon, 2000). Alternative assessment approaches have been sought that would identify students who need assistance at an earlier point in their education, guide the intervention process, and determine the intervention's effectiveness on the student's performance. These approaches have been called response to treatment (Heller, Holtzman, & Messick, 1982; Vaughn et al., 2003) or Response (Responsiveness) to Intervention (Barnett, Daly, Jones, & Lentz, 2004; D. Fuchs & Fuchs, 2005; Gresham, 2002; Mellard, Byrd, Johnson, Tollefson, & Boesche, 2004). Because the reauthorization of IDEA stipulated that establishing an intelligence-achievement discrepancy is no longer required to determine students with learning disabilities and that alternative research-based procedures must be permitted, many states are now in the process of phasing in RtI procedures (Berkeley, Bender, Peaster, & Saunders, 2009).

DEFINITION OF RESPONSE
TO INTERVENTION

Response to Intervention is a schoolwide process that integrates curriculum and instruction with ongoing assessment and intervention (E. Johnson et al., 2006). It is characterized by a multi-tiered or layered set of increasingly intensive interventions that are designed to enhance the early identification of students who exhibit deficits in basic skills so that they will not fall further behind other students (Bender & Shores, 2007; E. S. Johnson & Smith, 2008; Vaughn et al., 2003). The intent of RtI is for all students to receive high-quality, scientifically validated instructional practices in the general education classroom so that they achieve higher levels of academic and behavioral success (Campbell, Wang, & Algozzine, 2010; Mellard & Johnson, 2008). Two approaches to designing an RtI process have been described in the literature and implemented at the state and local levels: standard protocol models and problem-solving models.

Standard Protocol Models

Standard protocol models require the use of scientifically based classroom instruction with all students, regular administration of curriculum-based assessments, and frequent comparisons of students to expected or normal growth (D. Fuchs & Fuchs, 2005). If a student is not progressing as expected, he or she receives a well-defined intervention, which may be scripted. Because of the standardized nature of the instruction, practitioners are able to not only implement it with fidelity but also to determine that the student's unresponsiveness is not related to poor instruction or inadequate interventions.

For example, L. S. Fuchs et al. (2006) described a standard protocol approach in extending RtI to math problem solving. They provided the same curriculum to 40 general education classrooms. The "Hot Math" whole-class instruction occurred two to three times per week for 16 weeks for 25–40 minutes per session. It included four units that incorporated explicit instruction about transfer and self-regulation strategies. All of the problems were structured in the same way and teachers followed structured lesson plans. In addition, all students were assessed at the beginning of the school year, and some of the students, those who scored more than a standard deviation below the growth of their peers or below the 16th percentile, were placed in Hot Math tutoring, which occurred three times weekly for 13 weeks. The Hot Math tutoring occurred in groups of two to four students, three times per week for 13 weeks, each time for 20–30 minutes. The curriculum mirrored the whole-class sessions but more difficult concepts were targeted for instruction that used concrete manipulatives and extra prompts. They found that the Hot Math interventions in the general education classroom and in the tutoring sessions improved the performance of students on curriculum-based measurements. Those students who continued to be unresponsive were referred for more intensive services with highly skilled special educators.

Problem-Solving Models

In problem-solving models, the curriculum and interventions may vary depending upon the school or school district. A student's poor performance in the classroom will prompt a team-based examination of possible modifications, supports, or enhancements within the general education classroom (Kavale & Spaulding, 2008). The four-level problem-solving model generally involves (a) identifying the problem, (b) designing and implementing interventions, (c) monitoring the student's progress and modifying the interventions according to the student's responsiveness, and (d) planning the next steps (Bolt, 2005; Deno, 2002; Mellard et al., 2004). The model provides increasingly intensive interventions that are planned and implemented by school personnel. Referrals to special education services are made only in those cases where the suggested interventions are ineffective.

The problem-solving approach is also used within the schoolwide behavioral support model (e.g., Positive Behavior Support Model; Sugai, Horner, & Gresham, 2002). In this case, the interventions address behavioral concerns in addition to academic concerns. Similar to the academic problem-solving model, students are screened; the assessment information is compiled for review by the school's problem-solving team, which recommends appropriate interventions and supports for the individual student; the student's progress is monitored; and the problem-solving team makes decisions to continue, modify, or withdraw the intervention.

Four group-level problem-solving models that are consistent with RtI include Iowa's Heartland Agency Model (Ikeda, Tilly, Stumme, Volmer, & Allison, 1996), Ohio's Intervention Based Assessment (Telzrow, McNamara, & Hollinger, 2000); Pennsylvania's Instructional Support Teams (Kovaleski, Tucker, & Duffy, 1995); and Minneapolis Public School's Problem-Solving Model (Minneapolis Public Schools, 2001). Using the Heartland Agency Model, Bolt (2005) described how a kindergarten student's (Joshua) needs were addressed using a problem-solving approach. First, the school used the Dynamic Indicators of Basic Early Literacy Skills (DIBELS; Kaminski & Good, 1998) as a universal screener for identifying early literacy problems. Based on the results of fall and mid-year DIBELS scores and a teacher recommendation, Joshua and a small group of students who appeared to be at risk were provided instruction for 15–20 minutes a day, 4 days a week, across 5 weeks, using a program that had research support for teaching specific early literacy skills to young children. After this initial intervention, Joshua's progress continued to be discrepant from his peers. After a psychologist's observation, it was found that Joshua was not only discrepant from his peers in literacy skills but also in attention-related skills. Joshua was moved to an individual intervention that included a reading program delivered in 20-minute sessions three times a week and instruction on eye contact, which was monitored by the psychologist and reinforced by the classroom teacher. After 7 weeks of implementation, Joshua made substantial progress but was still behind his peers. At this point, the problem-solving team decided to assess Joshua's need for special education services. After being admitted as an "entitled individual," an Individualized Education Program (IEP) was established where he received one-on-one early literacy instruction daily by a special education teacher and his eye contact skills were monitored.

The majority of states use a combination of standard protocol and problem-solving approaches (Berkeley et al., 2009). Each of the approaches emphasizes high-quality instruction, the use of ongoing assessments in making decisions regarding the progress of students, and collaboration.

COMPONENTS OF RTI

Key components of RtI include (a) a strong general education curriculum, (b) a system for implementing research-based interventions at all tiers prior to formal identification with fidelity checks on implementation, (c) assessments that include universal screening and progress monitoring, (d) collaborative problem solving that allows greater involvement of parents and professionals, and (e) the use of professional development so that practitioners can implement the components of RtI (Hughes, Rollins, & Coleman, 2011; Johnson et al., 2006).

Strong General Education Curriculum

RtI is based on the principle that all children can learn and achieve high standards if given access to a rigorous, standards-based curriculum and research-based instructional practices. To develop a strong core curriculum, it needs to be aligned to rigorous, well-defined standards that are driven by postsecondary education and careers (e.g., PK–16 standards). Standards have been developed by most states, each of the major professional associations in core content areas, and more recently by the Council of Chief State School Officers (CCSSO), which developed a set of common core standards in English language arts and mathematics (CCSSO, 2010; International Reading Association & National Council of Teachers of English, 1996; National Council of Teachers of Mathematics, 2000). These standards were identified by practitioners and scholars based on their knowledge of the latest research in each of the content fields. In implementing the standards, educators need to be aware of the instructional practices that are also research based. Some of these practices have been identified by the Institute of Education Sciences' (n.d.) What Works Clearinghouse, which publishes practice guides that summarize the level of research support in a variety of topics (e.g., reading, math, science, student behavior, curriculum and instruction, classroom management) at different educational levels (e.g., elementary, middle, high school).

Effective practices in different domains, primarily reading and math, may also be found in the research literature. For example, effective interventions for students with mathematics disabilities include (a) instructional explicitness (didactic form of instruction); (b) instructional design to minimize the learning challenge (precise explanations, carefully sequenced and integrated); (c) strong conceptual basis; (d) drill and practice; (e) cumulative review; (f) motivators to help students regulate their attention and behavior to work hard; and (g) ongoing progress monitoring (L. S. Fuchs et al., 2008). Some of the other classroom practices that have been identified as effective with special education students include direct instruction (e.g., Carnine, Silbert, Kame'enui, & Tarver, 2004); self-regulated strategy instruction (De La Paz & Graham, 2002; Deshler et al., 2001); content enhancement instruction (e.g., Bulgren, Deshler, & Lenz, 2007); cooperative learning (D. Johnson & Johnson, 1994); Success for All (Slavin & Madden, 2000); peer tutoring (e.g., Jenkins & Jenkins, 1981); Classwide Peer Tutoring (e.g., Greenwood, Delquadri, & Hall, 1989) and Peer-Assisted Learning Strategies (D. Fuchs, Fuchs, Mathes, & Simmons, 1997); and mnemonics instruction (Fontana, Mastropieri, & Scruggs, 2007).

To ensure fidelity of implementation of the practices, they need to be incorporated into professional development and follow-up activities that include both peer coaching and materials support. For example, if teachers are to implement progress monitoring with students, they will need the assessments and also professional support in how to use them. Intervention practices are continually evaluated as practitioners collect ongoing assessment about their effectiveness with individual students. In this way, the core general education curriculum is not only built on standards and sound practices but is dynamic and individualized to meet each student's needs.

Tiers of Intervention

RtI often includes a tiered system of interventions, which become more intensive and individualized based on the tier. Although the number of tiers and their distinctiveness from one another may vary by school district or state, most include three (see Table 1).

Tier 1. Tier 1 is generally viewed as the "universal core program" (Council for Exceptional Children [CEC], 2008). The curriculum is "preventive" (Berkeley et al., 2009) because it is high-quality, research-based, and developmentally appropriate instruction (Campbell et al.,

Table 1
The Tier Process in RtI

	Tier 1	**Tier 2**	**Tier 3**
Curriculum	Strong core for all students	Targeted interventions, which are based on the core, for students not responsive to Tier 1	Targeted interventions including alternative curriculum for students not responsive to Tiers 1 and 2
Assessments	Universal (three times per year); benchmark and ongoing assessments	Ongoing assessments with curriculum-based measurement	Ongoing and dynamic assessments; comprehensive assessment to formally identify student for special education services
Teacher	General education	General education with supports from specialists (e.g., content, speech, special education)	General and special education (e.g., speech, physical therapists, behavior specialists)
Research-based intervention	Core curriculum	Remediation of specific skills deficits; delivered for 8–10 weeks, 4 days per week, at 30 minutes per session	Remediation of specific skill deficits with an alternative program; delivered for more than 12 weeks and based on student need
Location	General education classroom	General education classroom and various locations	General education classroom and various locations

2010). Tier 1 may include the teacher reteaching specific knowledge or skills, using jump-start lessons that prepare the struggling student for lessons that will be presented to the whole class at a later time, providing alternative or additional activities that present the knowledge or skills in a different way, and developing other types of activities that provide more time and practice to assist the struggling student. In the case of standard protocol approaches, Tier 1 may also involve whole-class reading instruction with scripted directions (Brownell, Sindelar, Kiely, & Danielson, 2010). Assessments often include universal screeners (three times per year), regularly scheduled benchmark assessments to ensure that adequate progress is being made in the general education curriculum (e.g., end-of-unit assessments, course assessments, school district assessments), and ongoing or curriculum-based assessments (e.g., curriculum-based measurement). Students who fall below the criterion on any of these assessments and are "nonresponsive" proceed to the second tier.

Tier 2. In Tier 2, more intensive instruction is provided to specific students who have not been successful in Tier 1. It is viewed as a "secondary intervention" (Berkeley et al., 2009) or "secondary prevention" (Reschly, 2005). The general education teacher and specialists who have received training in specific interventions may deliver instruction individually or in small groups within the general education classroom or in other settings, such as resource rooms, before or after school (Campbell et al., 2010). The intervention is generally delivered for a period of at least 8–10 weeks, 4 days per week, for 30 minutes per session. Instruction is focused on the remediation of specific skills deficits and may use a standard treatment protocol (scripted or partly scripted model), a problem-solving approach, or a combination of both. Students may receive various types of assistance in terms of differentiation, modification, adaptation, more specialized equipment, and technology (Hoover & Patton, 2008). Throughout the interventions, the student's responses are documented, which provide specific information for future decision making. The specialized training, together with the explicitness of the instruction and its empirical validation, the small and homogeneous student groups, and the greater frequency and duration of the tutoring sessions, make Tier 2 more intensive than Tier 1 (D. Fuchs, Fuchs, & Stecker, 2010). If the student responds to the intervention, then he or she may return to Tier 1, the core curriculum. If the student is unresponsive, then teams of educators combine their information to explore the student's eligibility for Tier 3 interventions (Fiorello, Hale, & Snyder, 2006; Hale, Kaufman, Naglieri, & Kavale, 2006).

Tier 3. Tier 3 interventions are targeted to those students who have not been successful in Tiers 1 and Tiers 2. Tier 3 descriptions are the most varied among RtI models. Some professionals consider this tier as representing formal special education services (D. Fuchs et al., 2010); others suggest that traditional special education may or may not be a part of this tier (Bradley, Danielson, & Doolittle, 2007); still others believe that special education is entirely separate from the RtI process

(CEC, 2008; Kavale, Kauffman, Bachmeier, & LeFever, 2008). In any case, Tier 3 does require a clinician who is trained in applied behavior analysis and has a deep knowledge of assessment and instruction. This clinician, whether a special and/or general educator, must be able to implement high-quality, intensive interventions systematically using a dynamic assessment process (test-teach-test) and continuously measure the child's progress (Deno, 1985; L. S. Fuchs, Deno, & Mirkin, 1984; Hoover & Patton, 2008). The interventions may take place in a wide range of possible educational settings, such as a special reading class or a resource room, over a period of more than 12 weeks on a daily basis (Campbell et al., 2010). If the student is responsive to the Tier 3 interventions, then he or she may return to Tier 2 or Tier 1. On the other hand, if the student is unresponsive, then the documentation from all of the interventions that have been used will serve as important prereferral information should more formal special education assessment be deemed necessary.

Brownell et al. (2010) described two examples of the RtI process in reading at the elementary and secondary level. For early reading, Tier 1 involves whole-class reading instruction that uses research-based practices focused on the essential components of reading. Tiers 2 and 3 target specific language deficits in reading and increasingly intensive ways of remediating them, with Tier 3 involving the most intensive instruction and frequent progress monitoring. At the secondary level, they described Deshler and Ehren's (2009) model, which incorporates well-structured general education instruction so that students learn the key ideas and concepts and cognitive strategies within and across content areas at Tier 1. Tier 2 is for those students who fail to comprehend content-area text and acquire the cognitive strategies. They would receive additional small-group intensive instruction designed to remediate skills in these areas for short durations of time. Students with more persistent problems would be provided with individualized instruction for longer durations (Tier 3). Instruction at this tier

> would likely include intensive cognitive strategy instruction, explicit instruction for understanding the vocabulary and linguistic structures of content area texts, and instruction in basic literacy skills such as fluency and spelling. It might also

incorporate assistive technology that scaffolds students' abilities to use strategies when reading or writing content area texts. (Brownell et al., 2010, p. 371)

Assessment

Assessment assumes a prominent role in RtI. It is used to determine if students are progressing as expected (i.e., universal screening) and to determine the effectiveness of curriculum and instruction (i.e., progress monitoring).

Universal screening. Universal screening involves assessments that are administered to the whole class at set times to identify students who are not progressing at the expected rate. For example, at the beginning of the school year, the teacher might administer curriculum-based measurement (CBM) instruments to examine basic skill proficiency. All of the students in the class might receive a word identification fluency test (i.e., the number of words read correctly in one minute) or a math problem-solving test (i.e., the number of math problems solved in one minute). Those students whose scores do not meet an established, empirically validated criterion (e.g., 50 words per minute at the first-grade level) would be monitored more closely to determine if they need more intensive services and if they were progressing at the expected rate. Other universal screeners might include standardized diagnostic screeners such as the DIBELS (Good & Kaminski, 2003) or school district benchmark tests that are aligned with the curriculum. The intention of all of the schoolwide screeners is to determine whether each student is likely to meet or not meet benchmarks and to find those students who need additional supports or individual interventions in order to succeed.

Progress monitoring. Ongoing academic and behavioral performance data are used to inform instructional decisions and improve student achievement. Direct and frequent samples of behavior before, during, and after implementing interventions provide the most meaningful information about how a student is responding and whether or not changes are necessary. These assessments need to be precise regarding the mastery of specific knowledge or skills, frequent, and sensitive to change (Ysseldyke, Burns, Scholin, & Parker, 2010). Commercial instruments such as Renaissance Learning and online tools such as CBMs are increasingly available for schools (Bryant et al., 2008; Chard et al., 2005; L. S. Fuchs, Fuchs, & Hollenbeck, 2007; VanDerHeyden, Witt, Naquin, & Noell, 2001). Other progress monitoring tools might include informal reading inventories, running records, observations, checklists, teacher-created probes, and conference interviews. Teachers may have freedom in creating curriculum probes and interventions, or they may receive explicit guidance and more structured formative assessments (Dorn, 2010). All assessments and interventions need to be documented to examine their effectiveness, note how often they are used, and ensure fidelity. In this way, current and future decisions are based on standardized approaches that can examine whether or not one set of intervention conditions are better than another for a particular student. In attempting to examine the effectiveness of interventions, D. Fuchs and Deshler (2007) have used the slope of improvement. If any students' level of performance and slope of improvement falls below the expected criterion or cut point, they are identified as nonresponsive and needing more intensive intervention.

Collaboration

Collaboration among educators, families, and community members is the foundation for effective problem solving and instructional decision making at each tier and increases the successful outcomes for students. The collaborative teaming process offers ongoing opportunities for parents, general educators, and special educators to share thier knowledge, experiences, and skills; evaluate data regarding the effectiveness of interventions; and generate novel interventions as needed. For the process to be effective, the team needs to meet face-to-face on a regular basis to monitor student progress and have a structure for addressing the issues. The team also needs to have a plan that assesses the implementation integrity of the intervention, must agree on responsibilities, and have clear individual accountability standards (Burns, Peters, & Noell, 2008; Hunt, Soto, Maier, & Doering, 2003; Turnbull & Turnbull, 2001). To support the collaborative process, the school needs to (a) determine who will teach students in the various tiers (e.g., general education teachers, special education teachers, reading specialists, speech-language therapists, paraprofessionals, other support personnel); (b) develop a structure for involving parents and families so that they are a part of team decisions and are notified when adjustments in instruction, levels of support, or educational services are made; and (c) provide time for collaboration to occur. The overall challenge for the collaborative team is to ensure that a seamless level of support exists among and across tiers so that all learners receive an appropriate education (Hoover & Patton, 2008).

Professional Development

Those who are involved in the RtI process need to have sufficient professional development, experience, and certifications to assume their roles competently and effectively. Table 2 shows some specific professional development needs for general education and special education teachers at each tier. Hoover and Patton (2008) have identified five roles and their corresponding skill sets that general and special educators must embrace in implementing interventions: data-driven decision maker, implementer of evidence-based interventions, provider of differentiated instruction, implementer of socioemotional and behavioral supports, and collaborator.

Data-driven decision maker. Educators need to know how to develop, use, and implement ongoing data-based systems such as curriculum-based measurement for monitoring students' academic performance and social-emotional development and making decisions about movement between tiers. Based on data, educators need to make decisions about the instructional level of the content they are teaching and the specific instructional approaches and modifications that will work best with each student. As the students progress through the tiers, educators need to be able to manage more frequent and precise monitoring. Moreover, educators who administer more formal, norm-referenced tests must possess appropriate training and credentials.

Implementer of evidence-based interventions. General and special educators need to be aware of evidence-based interventions and be amenable to implementing them. They need to consider which ones are effective in which content areas and for different students. For example,

Table 2
Needs for Professional Development

Tier	General Educators	Special Educators
1	• Teach general curriculum • Have knowledge of characteristics of students with disabilities • Create a positive classroom environment by teaching social skills • Assess and monitor student progress • Differentiate curriculum based on assessment information • Collaborate with parents and specialists as needed	• Have knowledge of general education curriculum, assessments, and data analysis • Use functional behavior assessment to develop preventive strategies • Collaborate with general education teachers as needed in adapting the general education curriculum
2	• Plan, implement, and evaluate more intensive interventions for students not succeeding in Tier 1 • Collaborate with parents and multidisciplinary team of specialists	• Have knowledge of interventions, technological adaptations, and assessments for students not succeeding in Tier 1 • Collaborate with parents and multidisciplinary team of specialists • Coteach with general education teachers as needed in adapting the general education curriculum
3	• Plan, implement, and evaluate more intensive interventions for students not succeeding in Tier 2 • Collaborate with parents and multidisciplinary team of specialists	• Have knowledge of intensive interventions, technological adaptations, and assessments • Collaborate with parents and multidisciplinary team of specialists • Develop Individualized Education Programs (IEPs) as needed • Provide direct services as needed

what intervention might a teacher use with a student who had difficulty in organizing information in mathematics versus reading? This information will support the implementation of high-quality core instruction (Tier 1), supplemental instruction (Tier 2), and intensive interventions (Tier 3).

Provider of differentiated instruction. Studies of general education teachers demonstrate that they have difficulty differentiating instruction for students with disabilities and other at-risk learners (Baker & Zigmond, 1995), especially at the secondary level (Mastropieri

& Scruggs, 2005). Educators need to know ways of differentiating curriculum and instruction not only with the whole class but also within small-group instructional settings. Differentiation includes the attention to individual differences in (a) what students need to learn (i.e., the content), (b) how much time they need to have to learn the content (i.e., pacing and rate), (c) how they learn the content (i.e., preferences), and (d) what environmental setting is best (e.g., small group, individually; Johnsen, Haensly, Ryser, & Ford, 2002). As students progress through the tiers, teachers need to learn how to provide more intensive, explicit instruction. Special educators also require a solid understanding of the general education curriculum in math, reading, and writing to enable them to teach students at all levels and to develop an instructional repertoire that integrates domain knowledge with intensive interventions and assessments.

Implementer of socioemotional and behavioral supports. Educators need to know how to create a positive learning environment that supports all students' learning. RtI models that address socioemotional and behavioral supports are based on principles of graduated systems and Schoolwide Positive Behavior Support (Lewis & Sugai, 1999; Sugai et al., 2000). At Tier 1, teachers need to learn how to recognize appropriate behavior in class, offer multiple opportunities for students to respond, minimize transition times, and provide direct and immediate corrective feedback (Fairbanks, Sugai, Guardino, & Lathrop, 2007). To implement Tier 1 and Tier 2 interventions, educators also need to have knowledge of applied behavior analysis and be able to conduct a functional behavior assessment to evaluate the classroom environment's effectiveness with each student (Sugai, Lewis-Palmer, & Hagan, 1998).

Collaborator. All educators require collaborative skills to engage successfully in the multidisciplinary planning needed for cohesive instruction at each tier. Educators need to know how to effectively interact with and support other educators in developing, implementing, and evaluating the effectiveness of interventions (Marston, Muyskens, Lau, & Canter, 2003).

Research evidence has demonstrated that general education teachers with special education preparation are better prepared to meet the literacy and mathematics needs of students with disabilities than teachers who lack it (Brownell et al., 2010). Preparation in special education has a value-added effect on the achievement of students with disabilities. Special education teachers also require a strong background in general education curriculum to make sure that instruction is cohesive at each tier level.

OPPORTUNITIES AND CHALLENGES

RtI presents both opportunities and challenges for educators. In terms of opportunities, RtI provides quality learning for all students because it focuses on implementing research-based curriculum and instructional practices. RtI also supports struggling students and helps them receive services before they begin to distinguish themselves through failure. It expands the roles of general and special educators and involves them in collaborative decision making regarding the quality and intensiveness of interventions. The descriptions of the student's response to intervention provides the team with more substantial information for communicating concerns with parents and making them a part of the problem-solving team. This team approach also develops a professional learning community within the school, which focuses on examining each intervention's effects so that ultimately instruction might be improved for all students. In addition, RtI uses resources more efficiently because common academic concerns are targeted.

On the other hand, RtI also presents a number of challenges. Research and validated protocols at the secondary level and in content areas other than reading and math are limited (D. Fuchs et al., 2010; McKenzie, 2009). There is also a restricted bank of interventions in some areas and many educators may lack in-depth knowledge on the ways of using protocols and interventions. Furthermore, interventions and behavioral consultations may not be equally effective in improving achievement when conducted by practitioners rather than researchers.

More work also needs to be done to identify measures for monitoring students' progress. Educators need to identify the types of assessments that provide the most useful information and that consider the cultural and linguistic differences among students. Even when teachers use technically adequate and instructionally sensitive assessments, they often lack a system for interpreting the data (Ysseldyke et al., 2010).

What does an expected growth rate resemble? When does a teacher need to intervene? Because some researchers have questioned the reliability of growth rates over multiple grade levels, what other ways are available for examining a student's progress (McKenzie, 2009)?

In practice, teachers perceive frequent formative assessment as a great paperwork burden and an addition to their already busy teaching load (Hasbrouck, Woldbeck, Ihnot, & Parker, 1999; Roehrig, Dugger, Moats, Glover, & Mincey, 2008). They are more familiar with planning lessons by discrete units of time (e.g., a 2-week unit on fractions) rather than planning lessons around assessments (Dorn, 2010). Assessment-driven decision making therefore takes teachers' time and energy and requires them to organize lessons not only for large groups but also small groups and individual students. Even when standard protocols are used, its top-down prescriptive nature grates on some teachers' sense of professionalism.

Because RtI models vary substantially with one another, some researchers urge caution in using assessments, even at the third tier, for the identification of students with learning disabilities (McKenzie, 2009; Vaughn et al., 2003). McKenzie (2009) stressed that nonresponsiveness and a specific learning disability are not always equivalent because a student with superior cognitive ability and a disability may still be able to respond. He also noted that assessments, which include error, are also susceptible to legal challenges against the school. Questions remain about where special education fits into the process. Is special education the third tier? If so, how are struggling students distinguished from those with a true learning disability? Will special educators work only with certified special-needs children? Will they use the general education curricula or specialized programs? Will they work within or outside the general education classroom?

Because it is clear the RtI process will change the roles of special and general educators, professional development will be needed for it to be successful. This will require preparation at the preservice, graduate, and in-service levels. Unfortunately, a recent national survey of special education preservice training programs indicated a paucity of structured collaboration content and collaboration (McKenzie, 2009). More educators need to be involved in preparing teachers and other professionals in implementing an effective RtI process.

SUMMARY

RtI is a federally mandated process that is most frequently used for identifying struggling learners and those with learning disabilities. It integrates curriculum and instruction with ongoing assessment and intervention within a multi-tiered process of increasingly intensive interventions. Standard protocol and problem-solving models are often used to design the RtI process, either individually or in combination. Components of RtI include (a) a strong core curriculum, (b) a tiered approach to implementing research-based interventions, (c) assessments that include universal screening and progress monitoring, (d) collaborative problem solving that involves parents and professionals, and (e) professional development for practitioners (Hughes et al., 2011; Johnson et al., 2006). Although RtI provides benefits for struggling students, such as immediate assistance and research-based interventions, it also presents challenges. These challenges include a restricted set of evidence-based interventions and assessments; a school culture that is based on time rather than assessment-driven decision making; errors in under- or overidentifying students with learning disabilities; a paucity of professional development at preservice, graduate, and in-service levels; and the lack of inclusion of gifted students with disabilities. This latter challenge will be addressed in the remaining chapters in this book. Where does the gifted student fit within an RtI framework?

CHAPTER

2

Strong General Education Curriculum for Gifted Students

A s mentioned in Chapter 1, RtI is based on the principle that all children can achieve high standards if given access to a strong core curriculum. To develop a strong core curriculum that includes gifted students, it needs to be aligned to evidence-based standards that are driven by postsecondary education and careers (i.e., PK–16 standards) and to standards in the professional fields. In implementing the standards, all educators need to be aware of practices in gifted education that are research based. This chapter will address standards and effective practices in gifted education that might be used within an RtI framework.

STANDARDS IN GIFTED EDUCATION

Similar to general educators, gifted educators use the content standards identified by major professional associations such as the National Council of Teachers of English (NCTE), the National Council of Teachers of Mathematics (NCTM), and so on as a basis for developing differentiated curriculum. In addition, CEC and the National Association for Gifted Children (NAGC) have developed teacher preparation standards and programming standards that identify these evidence-based practices of curriculum and instruction for students with gifts and talents (NAGC, 2010 [Standard 3]; NAGC & CEC, 2006 [Standards 4 and 7]).

Both sets of standards emphasize that the curriculum should be:

- aligned to local, state, and national standards;
- effective for students with talents across all domains (e.g., cognitive, affective, aesthetic, social, leadership);
- responsive to students from diverse backgrounds;
- comprehensive and continuous;
- defined by preassessment and formative assessment so that students' needs may be identified, differentiated education plans can be developed, and plans can be adjusted based on continual progress monitoring;
- adapted, modified, or replace the core or standard curriculum;
- advanced, conceptually challenging, in-depth, distinctive, and complex;
- paced, compacted, and accelerated based on the learning rates of students;
- individualized with technologies, including assistive technologies for twice-exceptional students; and
- integrated with career exploration experiences.

Along with these curriculum standards, NAGC and CEC (2006) included these specific evidence-based instructional strategies:

- independent research,
- metacognition,
- inquiry models,
- critical thinking,
- creative thinking, and
- problem solving.

The research base for these standards was comprised of empirical research, literature, and practice-based studies that supported each of the standards and its elements (Johnsen, VanTassel-Baska, & Robinson,

2008). More than 150 annotated summaries support the research base for the teacher preparation standards related to planning (Standard 7) and instruction (Standard 4; NAGC, 2006).

Models in gifted education incorporate many of these standards and may fit within an RtI framework, providing a strong general education curriculum for gifted and talented students.

TIERED MODELS IN GIFTED EDUCATION

In developing curriculum, gifted educators have proposed several models that are organized into three or more types, levels, or stages (see Table 3). These models include the Schoolwide Enrichment Model (SEM; Renzulli, 1977; Renzulli & Reis, 1985), the Purdue Three-Stage Enrichment Model (Feldhusen & Kolloff, 1986), and the Levels of Service approach (LoS; Treffinger & Selby, 2009).

Schoolwide Enrichment Model

The Schoolwide Enrichment Model consists of three stages of enrichment. Type I enrichment exposes students to a variety of topics that are not necessarily a part of the general education curriculum but motivate students to pursue new interests. Motivated students then pursue Type II enrichment, which consists of group activities in areas such as cognitive training (creativity skills, creative problem solving, critical and logical thinking), affective training (intrapersonal and interpersonal skills), learning how-to-learn training (observing, listening, note-taking, outlining), using advanced research skills and reference materials, and developing written, oral, and visual communication skills (Renzulli, 1994). Type III enrichment is for those students who pursue an in-depth study in a particular area of interest. Most often a specialist in gifted education guides this in-depth study, but for those students who are highly talented in a particular area, a mentor may be the best guide. In this way, the student can develop more professional levels of expertise in an area of interest.

This model easily fits into the tiered levels of service within an RtI framework (see Table 3). Type I and even Type II enrichment activities might be used with all students and provide general enrichment within

Table 3
Gifted Education Tiered Models Within an RtI Framework

	Tier 1	**Tier 2**	**Tier 3**
Schoolwide Enrichment Model	Type I and Type II activities with all students; preassessment and curriculum compacting	Type III activities with accelerated students who want to do in-depth studies	Type III activities for highly talented and accelerated students with mentors who can assist with professional levels of expertise
Purdue Three-Stage Enrichment Model	Stage 1 and Stage 2 activities with all students that emphasize divergent, convergent, and creative problem-solving skills	Stage 3 activities with accelerated students who want to do in-depth studies and produce complex products; inclusion of competitions such as Future Problem Solving Program International and Odyssey of the Mind	Stage 3 activities for highly talented and accelerated students with mentors who can assist with developing professional levels of expertise
Levels of Service Approach	Level I and Level II activities for all students that include exploratory experiences that allow students' strengths, talents, and interests to emerge and voluntary enrollment in activities to develop specific areas of interest	Level III activities that extend beyond the general education curriculum for some students who have documented skills and sustained interests	Level IV activities that extend beyond the general education curriculum for a few students who require highly individualized programs because they have an extraordinary level of skill development and commitment

the classroom. Although a specially trained gifted educator might orient the students to SEM, the general education teacher might also receive professional development in the design of enrichment activities so group-training activities could be implemented with all students. This model is often paired with curriculum compacting (Renzulli, 1994). With curriculum compacting, students are preassessed prior to instruction. Those students who have already mastered the content are allowed to pursue topics in greater depth within multiple settings (i.e., Type III enrichment).

Research on the SEM has shown that it is adaptable to a wide variety of school districts (Burns, 1998). Using SEM for reading enrichment, elementary students were exposed to books in their areas of interest, daily supported independent reading of challenging self-selected books using differentiated reading instruction, and interest-based choice opportunities in reading. When 5 hours of regular grouped reading instruction was replaced with short conferences and enriched reading based on interests, significant differences were found in reading fluency and attitudes toward reading (Reis et al., 2005; Reis & Fogarty, 2006). In another study comparing a direct instruction program with added remedial practice in the afternoon versus direct instruction with afternoon enrichment, students who participated in the SEM reading enrichment model scored statistically higher than the remedial practice group in both oral reading fluency and attitudes toward reading (Reis et al., 2007). In general, students who were able to participate in self-selected independent studies initiated their own creative products both in and outside school more often than nonparticipating students (Starko, 1986), improved personal skills such as perseverance (Delcourt, 1988), identified long-term interests (Delcourt, 1993; Taylor, 1992), and increased self-esteem (Olenchak, 1991). SEM also helped gifted students from special populations such as those with learning disabilities (Baum, 1988; Olenchak, 1991) and underachievers (Emerick, 1988). Gifted students with learning disabilities who completed Type III projects improved their attitudes about learning at both the elementary and high school levels and increased their self-esteem (Olenchak, 1991). Moreover, curriculum compacting studies showed that gifted students were able to eliminate up to 54% of the mathematics or language arts content with no differences in achievement (Reis, Westberg, Kulikowich, & Purcell, 1998; Renzulli & Reis, 1994).

Purdue Three-Stage Enrichment Model

In this model, Stage 1 focuses on developing convergent and divergent thinking skills and academic content within engaging units that emphasize verbal and nonverbal processes and fluency, flexibility, originality, and elaboration (Feldhusen & Kolloff, 1986). The goal of this stage is to enhance the student's thinking skills. Stage 2 encourages the development of Creative Problem Solving (CPS) abilities and learning within the CPS model, Future Problem Solving Program International, Odyssey of the Mind, and other inquiry-based models. Similar to SEM, the third stage involves gifted students in developing independent study skills, which could involve writing stories and producing plays.

Although this model is often implemented in a resource room for gifted students, many of the activities lend themselves to Tier 1 and even Tier 2 activities such as the development of divergent and convergent thinking skills and the incorporation of CPS into curricular units (see Table 3). The general education and gifted education specialists could collaborate in designing units that incorporated these types of thinking skills, which would allow gifted students to pursue content more deeply.

The three-stage model has its foundation in course development at the college level (Feldhusen, Ames, & Linden, 1973) and has been used in Saturday enrichment programs (Feldhusen & Sokol, 1982), future studies (Flack & Feldhusen, 1983), and in eight elementary schools (Feldhusen & Kolloff, 1986). Studies found that students who participated in the program developed more verbal and figural originality than students who did not (Feldhusen & Kolloff, 1986). Follow-up studies also indicated long-term effects. After surveying and interviewing seniors in high school who had participated in the three-stage model 6–9 years earlier, Moon and Feldhusen (1994) found that the students felt that their participation helped them succeed in high school and develop personal talent skills, self-awareness, and resilience.

Levels of Service Approach

The Levels of Service approach (Treffinger & Selby, 2009) is based on Treffinger's (1981) Individualized Programming Planning Model (IPPM). Similar to RtI, it is a needs-based model that looks for the best service options based on a student's characteristics. Options include differentiated basics; effective acceleration; appropriate enrichment; independent, self-directed learning; personal growth and social development; and career orientation with a futuristic perspective at increasing levels of intensity at four different levels.

Level I options contain services for *all* students and include exploratory experiences that allow students' strengths, talents, and interests to emerge. Activities include:

- differentiated basics that incorporate Bloom's taxonomy and exploration of talent areas into core curriculum;
- acceleration that allows each student to master the content at his or her own individual pace;
- enrichment, including general exploration, field trips, guest speakers, interest centers, and afterschool and Saturday programs;
- independent and self-directed activities stimulating small groups and individual students to conduct projects;
- personal and social growth activities to help students understand themselves and study interpersonal or group skills; and
- careers and future orientation activities, making students aware of change, futures, and careers.

Level II options contain services for *many* students and allow for student self-selection and voluntary enrollment based on student interest and competence in a specific area. Activities include:

- differentiated basics that allow students to explore interest areas beyond the core curriculum;
- acceleration that allows each student to test out of content he or she already knows;
- enrichment, including self-selected programs based on student interests, clubs and hobbies, Future Problem Solving Program International, Junior Great Books, and inventing;
- independent and self-directed activities stimulating small groups and individual students to conduct projects based on student interests as extra credit;
- personal and social growth activities incorporating simulations for students to explore special needs and involving students in varied roles in class or school projects; and
- careers and future orientation activities making students aware of careers and future issues and involving students in Future Problem Solving Program International.

Level III options contain services for *some* students who have documented skills and sustained interests. Activities often extend beyond the general education program and include:

- differentiated basics that allow students to advance beyond the core curriculum, learn more complex content, and participate in advanced courses;
- acceleration that allows each student to test out of content, including credit-by-exam, single subject acceleration, and talent search programs;
- enrichment, including investigations of real problems and challenges and small instructional groups for specific talent or interest areas;
- independent and self-directed activities extending students' current level of interest, knowledge, or experience giving them new opportunities to extend learning;
- personal and social growth activities incorporating leadership opportunities and involving small groups to address personal and interpersonal skills and tools; and
- careers and future orientation activities engaging students in programs such as Junior Achievement or other career- or future-related program opportunities based on students' interests, experiences, and applications.

Level IV options contain services for *few* students. These services are highly individualized and require an extraordinary level of skill development and commitment. Activities include:

- differentiated basics, including independently planned and managed programs or contracts for individual students;
- acceleration, including early admission, early graduation, grade advancement, and dual enrollment in courses at varied levels and sites;
- enrichment, including participation in special programs or projects away from school, mentorships, and advanced independent projects;
- independent and self-directed activities allowing students to do research/projects with mentors or organizations and high-level contests, competitions, or service projects;

- personal and social growth activities stimulating leadership roles in clubs or at the class or school level and participation in community activities and forums; and
- career and future orientation activities allowing students to participate in internships, job shadowing, and mentoring opportunities based on students' future personal and career goals.

Because this model is based on each student's need, it does not specify activities for general education, gifted education, or special education settings. Programming depends on each student's characteristics, interests, and experiences, which may vary for the same student across times and places. However, activities within Levels I and II might easily be a part of a strong general education curriculum (Tier 1) whereas Levels III and IV would need to involve gifted education specialists who would engage the students in services that are beyond the core curriculum.

Research supporting the various levels within this model is based on studies of talented people's lives (Bloom, 1985) and key elements of talent development (Selby & Young, 2001; Young & Selby, 2001). These key elements include helping students (a) become aware of and explore talent areas; (b) recognize the benefits of discipline; (c) be prepared to invest time, energy, and resources; (d) find support within and outside the school; and (e) be alert for transformational experiences (Selby & Young, 2003).

CURRICULUM MODELS IN GIFTED EDUCATION

In gifted education, there are also research-based curriculum models that provide a strong general education core for gifted students. These include the Integrated Curriculum Model (ICM; VanTassel-Baska, 1986) and acceleration models such as the Stanley Model of Talent Identification and Development (Stanley, Keating, & Fox, 1974).

Integrated Curriculum Model

The Integrated Curriculum Model has "three dimensions: (a) an advanced content focus in core areas; (b) high-level process and product work in critical thinking, problem solving, and research; and (c) intra- and inter-disciplinary concept development and understanding" (VanTassel-Baska & Wood, 2008, p. 213). The Center for Gifted Education at The College of William and Mary has developed units in math, language arts, social studies, and science that incorporate these dimensions and span grades 2–8. These units are based on the national standards and are used as models for schools in developing their own curricula (VanTassel-Baska & Brown, 2005).

Research from quasi-experimental and experimental studies has reported the units' effectiveness in increasing (a) students' literary analysis and interpretation, persuasive writing, and linguistic competency in language arts (VanTassel-Baska, Johnson, Hughes, & Boyce, 1996; VanTassel-Baska, Zuo, Avery, & Little, 2002); (b) students' integration of higher order process skills in science when embedding the units in exemplary science curriculum (VanTassel-Baska, Bass, Ries, Poland, & Avery, 1998); (c) critical thinking and content mastery in social studies (Little, Feng, VanTassel-Baska, Rogers, & Avery, 2002); (d) learning with low-income students when multiple units are used (VanTassel-Baska et al., 2002); (e) critical thinking and reading achievement for all groups of learners in Title I schools (VanTassel-Baska & Bracken 2006); and (f) student motivation when the units are used over a period of 3 years (VanTassel-Baska, Avery, Little, & Hughes, 2000).

Stanley Model of Talent Identification and Development

The Stanley Model of Talent Identification and Development provides a diagnostic testing-prescriptive instructional approach using assessments that discriminate with gifted students (e.g., above-grade level content, high ceilings). The assessment results are used to provide challenging curriculum, acceleration in core academic areas, and curriculum flexibility. Students who demonstrate that they have already learned the core grade-level content are able to advance to above-grade-level content within the general education classroom with their peers or be accelerated in single subjects (e.g., math) or an entire grade level as needed.

The research supporting the benefits of acceleration spans 27 years. A national report entitled *A Nation Deceived: How Schools Hold Back America's Brightest Students* focused on the benefits of acceleration (Colangelo, Assouline, & Gross, 2004). Researchers have found that (a) when compared with their nonaccelerated peers, accelerated students scored approximately one grade higher on achievement tests (Kulik & Kulik, 1984); (b) seventh- and eighth-grade students can learn the high school mathematics curriculum in a quarter to a third of the usual time (Bartovitch & Mezynski, 1981); (c) high school students learned biology, chemistry, or physics in 3 weeks (Stanley & Stanley, 1986); (d) math accelerated students took their first calculus course by grade 9 (Kolitch & Brody, 1992); and (e) acceleration benefits social and emotional adjustment (Benbow, 1991).

MODELS THAT FOCUS ON PROCESS SKILLS DEVELOPMENT IN GIFTED EDUCATION

Along with the tiered and curriculum models, several other research-based models focus on the development of specific processes or thinking skills. These include Schlichter's (1986) Talents Unlimited model and the Creative Problem Solving (CPS) model (Osborn, 1963).

Talents Unlimited

The Talents Unlimited model focuses on the development and direct teaching of specific thinking processes that were described by Taylor (1978), which include productive thinking, communication, forecasting, decision making, and planning. All of the thinking processes are embedded within content areas. The model includes instructional materials and an evaluation system for assessing thinking skills development for students in grades K–12 (Schlichter, 1986).

The model has been used successfully in general education classrooms in increasing students' (a) creative and critical thinking (Schlichter & Palmer, 1993), (b) cognitive complexity of interactions in the classroom (Friedman & Lee, 1996), and (c) performance on standardized achievement tests (McLean & Chisson, 1980).

Creative Problem Solving

The Creative Problem Solving model contains five stages: fact finding, problem finding, idea finding, solution finding, and acceptance finding (Osborn, 1963; Parnes, 1981; Treffinger & Isaksen, 2005). In the first stage, fact finding, students identify all they know about the problem and conduct research as needed. During problem finding, students list alternative problems and identify one that might be the best at solving the larger problem. During idea finding, students brainstorm as many possible solutions as they can think of that relate to the problem. During solution finding, the students actually identify the best solution using an evaluation matrix. Finally, during the acceptance finding stage, students plan ways to have their solution implemented. In the classroom, problems can be created from classroom situations, such as: "How might we recycle more paper in our classroom?" Problems can also be found within specific domains, such as: "Franklin Roosevelt faced many challenges arising from the Great Depression. What were the main problems and how might he have solved them?"

Although research is limited, the CPS process has been highly effective with (a) marginalized adolescent populations such as high school dropouts when used with career exploration and mentoring (McCluskey, Baker, & McCluskey, 2005); (b) second-grade students in increasing their learning opportunities (Chant, Moes, & Ross, 2009); and (c) second- and third-grade gifted students in increasing their figural and verbal creativity, verbal originality, and verbal flexibility (Harkow, 1996).

EFFECTIVE PRACTICES IN SPECIFIC DOMAINS

Effective practices in specific domains for gifted students, primarily the core subject areas, may also be found in the research literature. These effective interventions for students with gifts and talents include

(a) acceleration (Cross & Coleman, 1992; Kolitch & Brody, 1992; Ravaglia, Suppes, Stillinger, & Alper, 1995; Stanley & Stanley, 1986); (b) in-depth study of fewer topics (Cross & Coleman, 1992; Johnson, Boyce, & VanTassel-Baska, 1995; Lupkowski-Shoplik & Assouline, 1993); (c) inquiry-based learning (Moar & Taylor, 1995; Neu, Baum, & Cooper, 2004); (d) interdisciplinary and cross-disciplinary units of study (VanTassel-Baska et al., 1998; VanTassel-Baska et al., 1996); (e) applications to real-world problems (Bleicher, 1993; Cross & Coleman, 1992); and (f) interest-based curriculum (Reis et al., 2007). All of these practices might be implemented within the general education curriculum and enhance Tier 1 and Tier 2 interventions.

SUMMARY AND CONCLUSION

A strong general education core curriculum for gifted students needs not only to be aligned with national and state standards but also needs to be based on effective, research-based practices. This chapter has reviewed tiered models, curriculum models, models that focus on process skills development, and domain-specific practices in gifted education. Each of the tiered models provides activities that would enhance the curriculum in Tier 1 and Tier 2, which would primarily take place in the general education classroom. Within these models, special attention is paid to individual differences in content (e.g., its depth and complexity, its interest to students), how students learn the content (e.g., using divergent, convergent, and CPS skills), how quickly students learn (e.g., acceleration, curriculum compacting), and the quality of the products that are produced (e.g., complexity, professional quality). Similar to the tiered models, curriculum models focused on advanced and interdisciplinary content, high-level thinking, and acceleration. Specific models focusing on process skills development included Talents Unlimited and Creative Problem Solving. These two models could easily be integrated into the general education curriculum to enhance the performance of gifted students.

The incorporation of curricular models from gifted education is particularly important for twice-exceptional students (i.e., gifted students with disabilities). When an RtI system focuses primarily on students with deficits in basic skills, twice-exceptional students may be overlooked because their deficits may hide their gifts and vice versa (Pereles, Baldwin, & Omdal, 2011). These students need teachers who will implement a curriculum that is challenging for everyone and provide activities for each student's area of strength. If not, these students' needs might not be identified, and other students with early signs of advanced abilities might regress (Burns, Collins, & Paulsell, 1991).

Core general education practices need to be continually evaluated as practitioners collect ongoing assessment about their effectiveness with individual students. In this way, the core general education curriculum is not only built on standards and sound practices but is dynamic and individualized to meet each student's needs.

CHAPTER

3

Tiers of Intervention

· ·

According to the philosophy behind Response to Intervention, services at each tier should be based on student need rather than a student's label. This chapter will focus on gifted students and how they might be included within the intervention process. The following areas will be described for each tier: curriculum and services for gifted students for each instructional setting, the person responsible for services, assessments of learning, and the duration and goals used to determine placement.

TIER 1 INTERVENTION

Instructional Setting

Tier 1 takes place in the general education classroom with the full range of students in a classroom. According to the No Child Left Behind Act (NCLB, 2001), the core curriculum should be supported by scientifically based research and practices. It has been difficult to define the term *high-quality instruction* across practitioners in both general and gifted education, but most definitions include four concepts: rigorous content, differentiated instruction, cultural relevance, and social learning.

Rigorous content. When applied to general education curriculum, rigor refers to the depth and complexity of the content. Rigor consists of applying critical or creative thinking skills, such as those described in Bloom's taxonomy (Bloom, 1956) or in Creative Problem Solving (Osborn, 1963), to existing content or to a restructured curriculum that is more concept- or problem-based (Gallagher, Stepien, & Rosenthal, 1992; VanTassel-Baska & Little, 2011). Elements of good teaching, such as connecting new information to prior knowledge, using an organized sequence of instruction, linking assessment and instruction, and pacing lessons according to each student's needs, all contribute to the concept of rigor (Hoover, 2011). In order for the content to be considered rigorous for gifted students, the teacher should use ambiguous situations that are emotionally provocative or meaningful to gifted students. Each student is able to construct a personal understanding of the content that can be applied to real-world and ill-structured problems.

Although reformists often refer to a rigorous content, educational literature on this issue appears to support more rigorous instruction. Bloom's Revised taxonomy (Anderson & Krathwohl, 2001) and other thinking hierarchies (Ennis, 1985; Paul, 1990) offer a starting point for designing rigorous instruction that focuses on critical and higher level thinking. Basic skills may be taught at the knowledge level and students may be asked to remember this information on assessments, but these skills must be used in higher processes in order to produce more complex student outcomes. Gifted students need opportunities to practice critical thinking and problem solving in new situations (Krajcik, McNeill, & Reiser, 2008). All students are expected to master basic skills, but in a rigorous curriculum, basic skills are embedded in situations or practiced in settings that prepare students for professions and life outside the classroom. Skills such as collaboration and leadership should be included in the general curriculum and used to encourage the production of effective written and oral communication.

Differentiated instruction. Differentiated instruction is responsive instruction tailored to fit the needs of individual students. Differentiation requires using pre- and ongoing assessments to group students according to instructional needs or interests and to pace instruction according to how quickly each student learns the content. The groups are flexible because each new grouping is based on assessment results. By grouping students according to levels of prior knowledge and rates of learning, teachers can scaffold instruction within the *zone of proximal development* and create a moderately challenging instructional environment for all learners. The zone of proximal development represents the difference between what a student can do alone and what the same student can do with support (Vygotsky, 1978). Differentiation that reaches the level where a learner is moderately challenged but not frustrated lies within the zone of proximal development. In managing homogeneously grouped students, the teacher might choose to use tiered assignments, which vary the levels of tasks to ensure that students explore new ideas and use skills that encourage growth. Assignments may vary based on the required level of thinking, the abstractness of the content, the complexity of the resources, and the complexity of the student outcomes (Tomlinson, 1995). Within-class flexible grouping of students in elementary classrooms that is matched to each student's needs has been found to result in higher achievement for gifted and talented students with no negative effects for low achievers (Kulik & Kulik, 1992; Rogers, 1991; Slavin, 1987; Tieso, 2005).

Content, process, product, and instructional strategies all need to be differentiated in the classroom (Schiever & Maker, 2003). The content refers to what is taught in the classroom. All students should have access to the general education curriculum content, but students who are gifted in specific areas should also be able to bypass curriculum that they already know and access content that is above grade level and beyond what is included in the standard curriculum. The process, or how students think about what they are learning, follows the same logic. Some students will be applying basic skills while others will be developing new ideas that extend the content. Products and performances and other student outcomes should also be differentiated to maximize the potential of each student. These must be aligned to the content and the process in order to fully evaluate a student's learning. For example, on a rubric, the characteristics for using a specific research method might be more detailed and complex for a gifted student than for a student who is just learning to conduct research. Finally, the teacher's instructional strategies may vary for individuals or groups of students. Some students will benefit from direct instruction whereas other students may benefit from inquiry-based approaches or independent studies.

Differentiated instruction in the classroom will typically involve three levels of planning for content, process, and product. The initial level of planning should address curriculum standards for students who are performing on grade level. Content for this level includes examining the knowledge and skills in a content area. Instructional strategies may include modeling, direct instruction, guided practice, or other instructional techniques found to be successful with this group of students (Hoover, 2011). For example, students who are on grade level are expected to identify the main idea of a narrative essay. During direct instruction, the teacher models identifying the main idea and then leads the students through guided practice exercises resembling the modeled lesson. The students then complete independent practice based on the lesson.

Students who struggle with grade-level content will require a modified content, process, and product. For content, the teacher identifies the essential characteristics or the critical attributes of concepts to be taught in the lesson based on the preassessment results. These characteristics are then taught to the students through direct instruction and are used when designing the product or evaluation for the students. Conversely, students who are above grade level in one or more subject areas need to have the content, process, and product accelerated. If they already understand the knowledge and skills at their grade level, the content might be compacted, allowing them to pursue an in-depth study in an area of interest (Renzulli, Smith, & Reis, 1982). Instruction from the teacher might include guided questions and structural requirements for the independent research. Student learning in this case may be evaluated through a novel product or a presentation of the independent study.

Culturally relevant instruction. Culturally relevant instruction validates student heritage and backgrounds by forging a link between school and home life. It requires a wide variety of instructional techniques to ensure that all students achieve academically while maintaining a strong cultural identity. To understand culturally relevant instruction, it is important to understand the concept of culture. Culture provides the lens through which a group of people views the world (Ford, 2003). This lens is developed over time by the language, values, beliefs, attitudes, and experiences shared by the group. It is important to understand students in relation to their predominant cultural experiences because these experiences determine how a student responds to a given situation and, in turn, should guide the design of an appropriate curriculum and learning environment.

Ford (2011) described characteristics of a culturally sensitive learning environment for gifted students from diverse backgrounds as having (a) a curriculum that is culturally responsive and/or multicultural, (b) a teacher whose style is modified to match the learning styles of culturally different students, (c) assessments that are modified to accommodate cultural and language differences, and (d) partnerships with the family that are sensitive to cultural differences, issues, and needs. In addition, teachers need to ensure all cultures represented in the school are integrated across the curriculum. Mentor relationships with community members of the same culture might also be used to develop areas of expertise in gifted students from diverse backgrounds.

Social learning. The interaction between social factors and academic achievement has been well documented. For example, self-regulation competence initially develops from feedback from social sources and becomes internalized over time (Vygotsky, 1978). Internalized self-regulation appears to enhance levels of self-efficacy, which has been linked to academic achievement (Burney, 2008). For giftedness to develop, it needs a social environment that provides nurturance and guidance (Tannenbaum, 2003). A service-oriented curriculum that is paired with gifted students working together provides opportunities for growth in the social area.

Service learning allows gifted students to experience and address social issues that challenge idealism (Terry, Bohnenberger, Renzulli, Cramond, & Sisk, 2008). When the Tier 1 curriculum contains service-learning opportunities, all students will have the opportunity to practice cooperation in the process of addressing ill-defined problems. With service learning, more able students also have a vehicle for developing leadership skills and nurturing gifts or interests. For all students, service learning, such as the Developmental Service-Learning Typology, helps promote civic participation through solving complex social problems (Terry et al., 2008).

Cooperative learning in the most general sense refers to students working together to accomplish a goal (Mills & Durden, 2004). Cooperative learning may assume many forms but not all of these are beneficial for all students. Educators have championed many arguments for cooperative learning, but the research demonstrates that cooperative learning without differentiation may not contribute positively to educational outcomes for gifted students (Mills & Durden, 2004). Gifted students are more likely to benefit from cooperative learning when they are homogeneously grouped (VanTassel-Baska, 2004).

Party Responsible for Tier 1 Intervention

The general education teacher provides instruction for Tier 1. NCLB specifies that general education teachers must be highly qualified, which means the teacher must hold at least a bachelor's degree, have full state certification, and demonstrate competency in all subjects taught. Because general education teachers may not have any additional certificates in gifted or special education, they will want to collaborate with other specialists in modifying and accelerating the curriculum.

Assessment of Goals in Tier 1

Assessment in Tier 1 involves universal screening and progress monitoring. Universal screening should be conducted at least three times a year to identify students who may be in need of more frequent progress monitoring. The schedule for universal screening should be coordinated throughout the school, and the screening should be conducted at relatively equal intervals. Data from universal screening need to be entered into a database that is accessible to administrators, teachers, specialists, and school psychologists. The information gathered during the screening may be used to evaluate progress at several different levels. It can be used as a barometer of the district's progress toward year-end goals when all schools are assessed at approximately the same time, but it can also give an indication of individual campus progress. Teachers may use universal screening scores to evaluate whether their class is progressing appropriately. In addition, they may also look at individual student scores. The skills on a universal screening are based on what the average student should have mastered by the time of administration. According to this philosophy, approximately 80% of the students assessed should show mastery on the universal screening if it is a norm-referenced measure, and students should average about 80% correct responses on a criterion-referenced measure.

For gifted students, the universal screening instrument needs to include a higher level ceiling and address above-grade-level standards to identify students who may need to be accelerated. In this way, both students who are below grade level *and* students who are significantly ahead of their peers may be served (Hughes & Rollins, 2009). Addressing multiple grade levels is particularly important for gifted students who have learning disabilities. A universal screening instrument on grade level might be limited, as it may identify a student's weaknesses or disability but not his or her strengths or talents.

Progress monitoring, which is often confused with universal screening, takes place more frequently and is the foundation of RtI. When universal screening shows that a student is not performing as expected or is above grade level, the student is monitored weekly for a period of 5–6 weeks. Then, the teacher can use the data to make a decision about future programming. When scores from the universal screening show adequate grade-level progress, progress monitoring may be conducted less frequently. The frequency of progress monitoring will vary according to the needs of the student (e.g., weekly, monthly). Graphing the results of progress monitoring by class and by individual gives a teacher dynamic feedback about instructional efficacy.

Duration and Goals of Tier 1

All students should remain in Tier 1 unless they require interventions that are not compatible with general education instruction. Tier 1 comprises the base instructional tier of RtI and is designed to meet the needs of approximately 80% of the students. The goal of Tier 1 is to provide access to the general education curriculum while still meeting the instructional needs of individual students.

TIER 2 INTERVENTION

Progress monitoring and universal screening in Tier 1 identifies students who may need additional interventions. Students identified as "at risk" according to universal screening should be monitored weekly for a period of 5–6 weeks to determine if the universal screening score is an accurate reflection of current performance. If students continue to show reduced progress or a need for instruction beyond what is offered in the general curriculum, there should be changes in the curriculum and additional instructional strategies will need to be implemented. This level is considered a Tier 2 intervention.

Instructional Setting

Tier 2 interventions represent an addition to Tier 1 instruction and often take place in the general education classroom. Similar to Tier 1, data from progress monitoring and other forms of assessment may be used to group students according to need. Two types of interventions are typically offered as a part of Tier 2: standard treatment protocols and the problem-solving model.

Standard treatment protocols. Standard treatment protocols are small-group interventions designed to meet a specific need. Groups of four to seven students participate in these interventions, and each student receives the same standardized treatment. Interventions are usually delivered in 30-minute sessions with a frequency of three to five times each week. Similarly, gifted students may be cluster grouped and may receive specialized interventions such as highly accelerated content (e.g., sixth-grade math standards in the second grade). Delivery of the intervention can take place with the general education teacher in the general education classroom or entire grade-level interventions may be scheduled. For a grade-level intervention, students with similar needs from different classrooms may be grouped for Tier 2 instruction. Instructional specialists such as gifted and special education teachers may also deliver interventions to regular education classrooms.

Problem-solving model. When homogenous groups cannot be formed, a problem-solving model may be a good alternative. These models are created using data on a specific student and can be formatted to address any need. A multidisciplinary team designs the intervention so this model requires more personnel resources than the standard protocol model. Designing the intervention requires at least four steps:

- The student's need must be identified through universal screening or a referral based on progress monitoring or other forms of assessment. The multidisciplinary team must define the objective for the intervention and collect the necessary data to establish a need.
- The multidisciplinary team creates a hypothesis based on the available data to explain the student's need.
- The multidisciplinary team creates a multistep plan to address the student's need. This plan should include the types of formative assessments to be used, the goals of the intervention, a master schedule for assessment and intervention delivery, and the decision criteria for a successful intervention.
- The multidisciplinary team schedules a meeting to evaluate the plan. The team uses this meeting to review progress monitoring data and other assessments to judge the efficacy of the intervention at meeting the initial goals.

For a Tier 2 intervention to be effectively evaluated, careful attention must be paid to the types of goals created in the initial planning phases. Goals must be measureable and based on data if they are to inform decisions about the efficacy of an intervention (McDougal, Graney, Wright, & Ardoin, 2010). Interventions may be successful, but if the success is not quantifiable, then it is hard to determine if the goals have been met. To be measureable, goals should specify the specific academic and/or social behaviors, the measurement conditions, and the level of performance required as a criterion (McDougal et al., 2010).

For gifted students, Tier 2 includes homogenous grouping within the general education classroom or across-grade-level groups that meet on a daily basis. For example, students who are in different classrooms but are all working on similar content that is several grade levels above their peers may be grouped together for instruction. Groups consisting of more able students not only meet academic needs but also provide the opportunity for students to learn from one another, to socialize with others who have common interests and abilities, and to develop knowledge about themselves (Burney, 2008; Plucker & Stocking, 2001).

Tier 2 small-group instruction needs to provide the appropriate level of challenge for a group of gifted students. When tasks are adequately challenging within the zone of proximal development, the optimal environment is created for developing self-regulation skills, such as persistence and emotional control (Burney, 2008), and a learning orientation, which enhances motivation and self-efficacy (Dweck & Leggett, 1988). To ensure the development of intrinsic motivation, tasks should also be interest-driven and allow for long-term engagement (Csikszentmihalyi, 1988).

Party Responsible for Tier 2 Instruction

The general education teacher or an instructional specialist such as a general, gifted, or special education teacher can administer instruction in Tier 2. The decision should be made according to the strengths of each teacher and the needs of the instructional group. Although general education teachers may be highly qualified in a content area as specified under NCLB, this does not mean that all general education teachers feel competent in delivering a specialized intervention for gifted students or those who are struggling learners. Multidisciplinary teams should choose the person responsible for the intervention based on several criteria: qualifications in area of intervention, past experience in implementing the intervention, and training in progress monitoring and other assessment procedures.

Assessment of Goals in Tier 2

For special education students, the ultimate goal of Tier 2 instruction is to return the student to Tier 1 instruction. However, gifted students may need a longer intervention if the general education teacher is unable to provide a specialized, accelerated curriculum on a daily basis. To evaluate this goal, progress monitoring on both growth and level of achievement should be collected weekly or twice weekly. Struggling students may achieve the growth goal of Tier 2 interventions but still remain in Tier 2 intervention because their ongoing level of performance demonstrated does not support a return to Tier 1. If a student's performance appears similar to Tier 1 expectations, then he can return to Tier 1; however, this student should be monitored closely to determine if achievement continues at an appropriate pace in the general education classroom. On the other hand, if a gifted student's growth exceeds the goals set in Tier 2, she may need to move on to Tier 3 services.

Because Tier 2 represents a more intensive intervention than Tier 1, progress monitoring is conducted more frequently. The data from progress monitoring are used to calculate the growth of students over time. The person performing the intervention is often the same person responsible for collecting and graphing the data related to progress monitoring. After collecting six to eight data points through progress monitoring, the interventionist should be able to determine a trend in student performance. Comparison between this trend and the aim line, or expected progress based on national, local, or gifted norms, helps determine if a student is making adequate achievement growth in the current intervention. If the student is not showing adequate growth (i.e., the struggling learner's data points indicate that he or she will not reach grade level by the goal date; the gifted learner's data points indicate that he or she is not accelerating above grade level at the expected rate), error analysis of the progress monitoring may help refine the intervention to accelerate growth. Figure 1 shows an example of a progress chart with an aim line based on national norms.

Graphs for progress monitoring may be constructed in statistical programs or other spreadsheet applications like Excel. It is important to chart the progress according to time such that the y-axis represents the behavior under progress monitoring and the x-axis represents time. Time should be divided into equal intervals that match the frequency of progress monitoring. Student data are plotted as a function of the behavior over time, so that each data point represents the intersection of performance on a particular date. Connecting the first and last progress monitoring data points with a line shows the trend of a student's growth and creates a trend line.

Construction of the aim line is contingent upon the norms used and the baseline performance of the student being monitored. The student's baseline, or first point in the aim line, is collected either during the first administration of the progress monitoring tool or from the universal screening. The last point used to construct the aim line is the goal

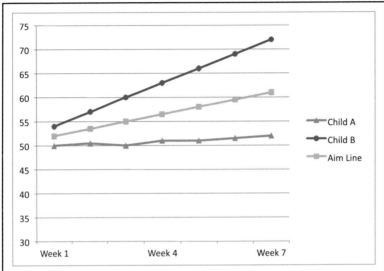

Figure 1. Reading progress chart. The aim line, indicated by the line with square markers, shows the expected rate of growth for a third-grade reading curriculum-based measurement (CBM). The aim line shows that students should gain approximately one new word each week of instruction. Child A, indicated by the line with triangular markers, is growing slower than expected. The slope of Child A's line is less than the slope of the aim line showing the student is in need of an intervention. The line with the circular markers shows progress for Child B. The slope of Child B's line is much greater than the aim line, so this child is progressing at a faster rate than the average student and may be in need of acceleration.

according to expected achievement and is usually taken from local or national norms. Connecting these two points establishes an aim line and student progress can be compared to this line when evaluating growth.

The student progress, determined by the trend line, may be compared to the aim line, and the result may be used to determine the next instructional step. If the trend line is flatter, or the slope of the trend line is less than the aim line, then an instructional change needs to occur. The current intervention is not producing the effects necessary for the student to reach the achievement goal in the specified time period. If the trend line slope is equal to the aim line slope, then the student is achieving as expected and should theoretically reach the achievement level desired. In this case, the intervention is working and should not be changed. If the trend line slope is greater than the aim line slope, then the intervention is working better than expected and the student may be able to exit Tier 2 before the specified date.

Duration and Goals of Tier 2

The duration of a Tier 2 intervention depends on the goals, or decision rules, adopted by the multidisciplinary team. The decision rule, created by the multidisciplinary team at the start of the intervention, specifies the criteria for remaining in or exiting Tier 2. Tier 2 should be considered supplementary instruction based upon the general education curriculum for struggling learners or a different curriculum for gifted learners, so it is feasible for a student to remain in Tier 2 throughout an entire year. This may not be possible due to a shortage of resources. In this case, alternate methods of intervention delivery can be explored. The time frame for Tier 2 depends on the emerging needs of the student, but initially the multidisciplinary team should set it. A 6–8-week intervention should provide enough instructional support to judge the efficacy of a particular intervention. Typically, the decision to exit Tier 2 is based on level of achievement and rate of progress.

TIER 3 INTERVENTION

Tier 3 intervention may be considered special education or gifted programming. It is implemented when the student is classified as a nonresponder or above-level responder to Tier 1 and Tier 2 instruction according to the decision rules created by the multidisciplinary team. For Tier 3 to be successful, several mechanisms need to be in place and functioning efficiently. These include identifying individual student needs and determining goals related to meeting the needs of an at-risk, high-achieving, or gifted student.

Instructional Setting

The instructional setting for Tier 3 is small-group instruction outside of the general education classroom. In special and gifted education models, this may be analogous to a resource room or a pull-out program. Instruction may occur with individual students or in groups as large as 10, depending on the age and need of the participants. Older students may be successful in large groups, whereas younger students may perform better in an individual or small-group setting. The same applies to the needs of the students: The greater the need is, the smaller the instructional group should be.

The instruction at this level is comprised of scientifically based, individualized interventions. Students in Tier 3 are determined to be non- or above-grade-level responders to the general education curriculum and Tier 2 interventions. Although the interventions at Tier 3 may be related to the core curriculum, the intensity, delivery process, and accommodations should be different than the modes typically found in the general education classroom. Instruction at the level is individualized based on data from prior progress monitoring and findings from a comprehensive evaluation. For special education, a combination of direct instruction and strategy instruction provides students with the academic and metacognitive skills necessary to perform in regular education. For students with gifts and talents, a combination of acceleration and enrichment might be necessary to address their interests and needs.

For students who achieve below the expected level and rate of progress in Tier 2, this may constitute a referral to special education and placement in a resource classroom. Instruction in a resource classroom includes many components shown to be effective with students with learning disabilities such as direct instruction (Mellard & Johnson, 2008). Resource classrooms use the content from the general education curriculum to set performance standards to help remediate deficient skills and prepare students to reenter the general education classroom (Mellard & Johnson, 2008).

Gifted or more able students may need a different type of Tier 3 instruction. Although the process of individualizing instruction may be similar, the types of instruction delivered may be very different. Students who show precocity in a specific skill or domain could be placed in a Tier 3 intervention designed to radically accelerate instruction in a single area. Acceleration can assume many different forms based on the pace and level of acceleration. In Tier 3, acceleration may assume the most intense levels and pace.

When a student's cognitive development outpaces the interventions available at the current grade level, the student's level of readiness may be more appropriately served in classrooms in a higher grade level (VanTassel-Baska, 2004). Allowing students to complete more than one year's curriculum in single instructional year, referred to as telescoping, may be appropriate for these students. Gifted students, even those in middle or elementary school, may benefit from Advanced Placement classes that offer dual high school and college credit so that they may be eligible for early high school graduation. Early graduation allows for early entrance to college, and many of the interventions used with these students in high school may apply to education at the postsecondary level.

Independent research represents another intervention within Tier 3. Using Treffinger's (1986) individualized programming planning model, Tier 3 instruction can be individualized to fit the needs of any gifted student through six foci: individualized basics; appropriate enrichment; effective acceleration; independence and self-direction; personal and social growth; and career and future aspirations. To tailor this model to individualized independent research, the gifted teacher in Tier 3 can address each focus through the lens of the student's current interest.

Part of the individualized nature of Tier 3 is the emphasis on independence and self-direction, so that students learn the principles of self-directed learning, when cognitively appropriate (Merriam & Caffarella, 1999). Reflection and communication with more advanced others, like mentors and role models, may lead to personal and social growth (Vygotsky, 1978). Exploring moral issues and ethics may be especially good topics for these reflections. The self-awareness developed through independent research and relationships with mentors may help students develop an appropriate set of future and career aspirations based on a thorough assessment of strengths and weaknesses.

In summary, the intensive level of interventions for gifted students may include radical acceleration, dual enrollment, early entrance to college, long-term research and mentorships, specialized counseling, and attendance at specialized schools.

Party Responsible for Tier 3 Instruction

In Tier 3, a specialist should deliver instruction. According to NCLB, the specialist must be highly qualified in specific content areas. Special education teachers also need to hold a certificate or license in the state in which they practice. Although qualifications for teachers in gifted education vary among states, they should meet the national teacher preparation standards in gifted education (NAGC & CEC, 2006).

Assessment of Goals in Tier 3

Planning Tier 3 interventions often requires information from a diagnostic assessment. For struggling learners, this may constitute the initial referral for special education. A multidisciplinary team should be assembled to make decisions about placement and interventions. If an evaluation of all existing data supports the need for additional information on academic or behavioral needs, then the student will be given a comprehensive diagnostic assessment. This type of assessment isolates specific academic and behavioral needs that may be used to design an individualized intervention.

Gifted students in Tier 3 may also need a comprehensive diagnostic assessment to determine a pattern of strengths and weaknesses that can be used to structure an individualized intervention. The assessment information may be used to create individualized instruction, an accelerated curriculum to meet the student's specific needs, or referral to a specialized program for gifted and talented students. Based on the strengths and weaknesses, a gifted student with disabilities may need remediation in some skills and acceleration in others.

All students in Tier 3, regardless of the reason for placement, should receive continual progress monitoring. The multidisciplinary team should determine the frequency of the progress monitoring, but research recommends daily progress monitoring (McDougal et al., 2010). Assessment of progress monitoring should use both rate of progress and level of achievement. Students in Tier 3 for remedial instruction need to achieve a level commensurate with the general education classroom. At this point, the student may be returned to Tier 2 for a less intense intervention.

Gifted students placed in Tier 3 should receive not only progress monitoring but also nontraditional assessments that can examine more complex products and performances. Progress monitoring should occur frequently, even daily, and should ensure that the students are achieving above grade level and at a rate of growth that exceeds the general education classroom. Rubrics should be used to determine if gifted students are developing professional quality products and performances. These assessments ensure the students' individual needs are being met by the intervention in Tier 3.

Duration and Goals of Tier 3

The duration and goals of Tier 3 are contingent on the needs of each student. Some students will remain in Tier 3 until a specific need is met and then return to a less intense tier of instruction; however, other students may remain in Tier 3 due to specific needs that cannot be met in the general education classroom. Progress monitoring determines when Tier 3 interventions are no longer necessary. Gifted students receiving Tier 3 interventions may continue to receive these interventions indefinitely if the need cannot be met in a less intensive tier. Needs like radically accelerated instruction associated with early college entry or grade skipping may require indefinite Tier 3 placement, but less intense needs like curriculum compacting in a single subject may not warrant continual placement in Tier 3.

SUMMARY

Interventions in RtI allow instruction to be based on the student needs revealed through progress monitoring. In Tier 1, rigorous content and differentiated instruction ensures access to a high-quality core curriculum for all students. Differentiation may be used to address the needs of some gifted students in the regular classroom by adjusting the content, process, and product in the core curriculum to fit specific student needs. When the needs of students cannot be met under Tier 1, then Tier 2 offers more targeted interventions with small-group instruction in the general education classroom. The instruction in Tier 2 can be targeted to meet the needs of relatively homogenous groups of students and may provide gifted students an opportunity to pursue interests that build on the core curriculum. Some students will need more individualized instruction and will benefit from content beyond the core curriculum. These students can be best served in a Tier 3 intervention, which uses independent studies, curriculum acceleration, and other techniques used to serve the highly gifted. The three tiers of RtI offer multiple opportunities to serve the needs of all students including the gifted.

CHAPTER

4

Monitoring Student Progress

• •

S chools collect a large variety of data on students. Some data, like demographic information, are used to understand trends in mobility, neighborhood characteristics, and other areas that may help develop an understanding of the school population. These data can be used longitudinally to plan for changes in the population and resource allocation. Schools also collect data on academic achievement of students that may be used to support an RtI framework. The key to data collection is using the information to create a challenging educational environment that is supportive of all learners, including those who are gifted and talented.

ASSESSMENT

Assessment is a process used to gather information for a specific purpose. In Response to Intervention, the assessment process is used to make decisions about specific curriculum needs and instructional strat-

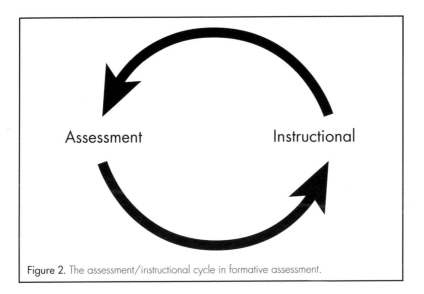

Figure 2. The assessment/instructional cycle in formative assessment.

egies for individuals or small groups of students, which may be a different use than what is familiar to most teachers. As shown in Figure 2, formative assessment allows teachers to design responsive instruction.

In a traditional assessment model, teachers often use summative assessment. A summative assessment is meant to show what a student has or has not learned and is often considered a deficit model (Riccomini & Witzel, 2010). Examples of summative assessments include benchmark exams, state assessments, semester exams, and chapter tests. They are designed to gauge students' learning against a set of criteria established by the content of the course. Summative assessments are useful for grading, program evaluations, curricular alignment, and formation of schoolwide goals.

The examples of summative assessments could also be considered examples of formative assessments; however, the application of formative assessment results is very different. Whereas a summative assessment is meant to gauge learning at a specific point in time, a formative assessment is used to inform instruction. An RtI model requires the use of formative assessments because the results of the assessments become an integral part of the instructional process. A formative assessment is generally used for feedback rather than a grade, and summative assessments are often used to assign a grade or ranking to students based on the results.

An RtI framework typically uses three types of formative assessments: universal screening, progress monitoring, and diagnostic assessments. Each of these assessment types plays an important role in decisions made within the RtI framework. With gifted children, the application of each type of assessment may differ from what is typically used in an RtI model that focuses on struggling learners.

Universal Screening

A universal screening instrument is central to the implementation of RtI and functions as a preventative measure. It is considered preventative because the purpose of the universal screening is to identify learners who may need additional interventions and assessments (Mellard & Johnson, 2008). Performance on the universal screener should be related to performance on high-stakes or state testing and as such should contain a sampling of the material tested at the end of the school year. Universal screening occurs three to four times each year at routine intervals with all students (Mellard & Johnson, 2008). Because the screening is repeated, it is essential to choose universal screenings that are quick, low-cost, and may be group administered.

The inclusive nature of universal screening makes it an ideal method for identifying gifted students from traditionally underrepresented groups and nurturing the potential in these students through early intervention (Coleman & Shah-Coltrane, 2011). Universal screening is often thought of as a way to identify students at risk for failure, but it also may be used to identify students in need of greater challenges. To accomplish this goal may be difficult, but a well-designed instrument will eliminate many of the barriers to simultaneous identification.

The choice of universal screenings should be made according to the needs of the school. Most schools will need a cheap, practical, and fast measure that can accurately determine students in need of intervention. Additionally, the measure should have a high test-retest reliability based on short intervals between testing, which would indicate that the universal screener is able to detect small changes in the construct being measured (Miller, Linn, & Gronlund, 2009). Universal screen-

ings identify students who need additional assessment, such as progress monitoring, and the design of a universal screening should reflect
this use. The universal screener should align with local standards and to
ensure the alignment, many schools choose to administer curriculum-
based measurements (CBMs) as universal screeners (VanDerHeyden &
Burns, 2010). Typically, CBMs provide direct measurement of local curriculum and reliably predict future performance. Because the goal of the
universal screening is to determine if a student will be successful with
Tier 1 instruction in the general education classroom or will require a
more intensive intervention, reliability and validity of the CBM must be
considered.

Reliability applies to the consistency of results from a measurement
and, with a CBM, test-retest reliability is especially important. Results
that demonstrate high test-retest reliability, such as correlations above
$r = .80$ between results from multiple administrations, allow educators
to assume that changes in the score are reflective of learning and not
variation due to the nature of the instrument (Miller et al., 2009). A correlation indicates how much the two scores have in common, so a correlation of $r = .80$ would indicate that results from the different administrations share 64% of variability, which leaves 36% of the variation in
scores unexplained. These numbers show that the higher the test-retest
reliability, the more confidence the teacher can have in the results over
time. When a change occurs in scores from separate administrations,
the test-retest reliability tells the teacher how likely the change is due to
learning.

If more than one form of a CBM is used for universal screening,
then equivalent forms reliability becomes an important consideration.
Each form of the CBM should consistently measure the same aspect of
behavior so the result from different forms administered to the same
student should correlate. As with test-retest reliability, the higher and
more positive the correlations are between different forms, the more
confidence a teacher is able to have with scores from equivalent forms.
Correlations above $r = .80$ are preferable for equivalent forms of CBMs
(Miller et al., 2009).

The accuracy of any measure is related to the psychometric properties of validity and reliability. In the case of universal screening, the measure should err on the side of false positives (VanDerHeyden & Burns,

2010). Students who are incorrectly identified as needing an intervention, evidenced by a false positive, will be discovered through the progress monitoring process, but allowing for high false positives makes it unlikely that students who need interventions will be missed by the universal screening. Adjustments made to the screener based on data collected through repeat administration and progress monitoring may help fine tune the universal screening such that a balance between accuracy and efficiency may be found (VanDerHeyden & Burns, 2010). For example, data collected over a 2-year cycle can be used to understand the patterns of misclassification occurring with a universal screening. If the screening misclassifies too many students as needing an intervention, then the screening may be too conservative of a measure, and adjustments can be made to the content or administration time so that results provide a more accurate means of classification.

Error analysis of this kind can also be used to adjust ceiling and floor effects that occur with specific groups of students, particularly gifted students. If the CBM had ceiling effects, it would not be able to identify more able students because these students would make perfect scores on the universal screening. A ceiling effect would indicate the need for adding more difficult items to the screening instrument. If the CBM had floor effects, then the instrument would not be able to discriminate between less able learners, indicating the need to add easier items.

Adjustments made to the universal screener may provide a balance between specificity and sensitivity, but the needs of the school may determine the exact nature of this balance. Sensitivity of a measure refers to the probability that the universal screening will correctly identify students needing an intervention (National Research Center on Learning Disabilities [NRCLD], 2006). On the other hand, specificity refers to the probability that a universal screening will not identify students who perform satisfactorily on a criterion measure at a later point in time—those who are truly not at risk (NRCLD, 2006).

Another consideration for universal screenings is how the screening should be scored. Most instruments fall into two categories: norm-referenced measures and criterion-referenced measures (VanDerHeyden & Burns, 2010). A norm-referenced measure compares results against a norming sample of typically developing peers (Miller et al., 2009).

In this way, results from the screening are compared to what would be considered average for the group of students tested. If a student's results deviate from this average, then the student may be identified as needing an intervention. Typically, norm-referenced universal screenings are not used because the results do not offer feedback on specific needs; however, using a norm-referenced screening may be useful when identifying more able students. To use the instrument for this purpose, the teacher or administrator would need to determine how different an individual's score is from the average score. If the student's score falls at least one or two standard deviations above the average score, then this student could be considered more able and may need additional interventions (Mellard & Johnson, 2008).

The criterion-referenced universal screenings are designed to measure performance against a set of predetermined criteria. By comparing a student's performance to a set of criteria, the universal screening can identify the areas of weakness and strengths more effectively than the norm-referenced screening. This approach would be particularly important for identifying gifted students who also have disabilities. Criterion-referenced screenings are also helpful in designing interventions for all learners. A student's strengths and weaknesses on this type of assessment can be used to differentiate the core curriculum to target specific needs. The majority of students will display both strengths and weaknesses, but unless the strengths and weakness are beyond what can be addressed in the general education classroom through appropriately differentiated curriculum, there is no need to consider alternative tiers of instruction.

How to use a universal screening in practice. The first step in using a universal screening instrument is selecting the instrument based on the criteria discussed in the previous sections and the content the school wishes to screen. The universal screening instrument should include content the average student should have mastered at the time in the year when the screening is administered (VanDerHeyden & Burns, 2010). A good way to identify the content for a universal screening is to look at the local standards and create a measurement based on what the standards indicate students should know at the time of the screening. The results from a screening may be used to make diagnostic decisions about the efficacy of Tier 1 instruction. For example, if the standards show that students should be able to perform a specific skill at the time of the universal screening and the majority of students are unable to perform the skill on the screening, then the results may be indicating a problem with the alignment between Tier 1 instruction and the local standards (VanDerHeyden & Burns, 2010). The results could be interpreted as a class-, grade-, or school-level problem with alignment between learning outcomes and standards. In this case, the general education curriculum needs to be evaluated for weaknesses. The opposite problem occurs when too many of the students show proficiency on the universal screening. This may show that the instruction in Tier 1 is highly effective and students may benefit from acceleration.

When the distribution of scores on a universal screening reflects a positive or negative skew, additional screening may be necessary. If too many students perform poorly on the screening, it will be impossible to discriminate between those needing an intervention and those who do not. This is referred to as a floor effect because the measure does not correctly classify individuals who score on the low end of the distribution. When this occurs, the students should complete a period of instruction and be reassessed with a different instrument. A ceiling effect, which is the opposite of floor effect, occurs when the measurement is not challenging enough to discriminate between high-achieving students. Ceiling effects are problematic when using RtI to identify high-achieving students who need additional instruction.

Gifted students and universal screening. A universal screening can be used to identify students who may benefit from instruction beyond the core curriculum. As discussed previously, ceiling effects could be a barrier to identifying more able students through universal screening, but the addition of above-grade-level content may add to the discriminative power of the instrument. Variability in content on the universal screening can be thought of as related to differentiation in the curriculum. Content from at least two grade levels above the current level of instruction may offer a method of identifying academically able students who may need Tier 2 interventions or more frequent progress monitoring.

Progress Monitoring

Progress monitoring has two main purposes: (a) identifying students who are not benefiting from the current level of instruction, and (b) providing information for the design of appropriate interventions (Mellard & Johnson, 2008). It should occur at all three tiers of RtI, and the measures used for progress monitoring should be taken from the curriculum used in the tier. Progress monitoring differs from universal screening because progress monitoring provides achievement data on a more frequent and routine interval. For example, universal screening may occur three times a year but it is recommended that progress monitoring be conducted on at least a monthly basis (Mellard & Johnson, 2008). Research supports adjusting the frequency of progress monitoring in relation to the intensity of the intervention, such that in Tier 1 the frequency would be much lower than in Tier 2 (VanDerHeyden & Burns, 2010). This allows instructional changes to be implemented before a student experiences failure in the regular education classroom and allows for ongoing acceleration for more able learners.

The general education teacher generally conducts progress monitoring at Tier 1. The data collected on students can be made available to instructional specialists and administrators through a common database. The general education teacher maintains graphs of student and class progress, which are then used to make timely curricular adjustments. The curricular adjustments are based on decision points set prior to the administration of progress monitoring.

In an RtI framework, progress monitoring should accomplish a multitude of goals. Primarily, it should assess skills evident in the state and local standards and be able to detect small changes in these skills (VanDerHeyden & Burns, 2010). In addition, progress monitoring should be efficient to administer, easily interpretable, and created for repeat administration to track progress over time. The goal of progress monitoring is to determine if a student is benefiting from instruction in the current intervention and as such, it is a valuable tool for making data-based decisions within the RtI framework. To be effective in meeting these goals, progress monitoring should occur at least monthly and the frequency should be adjusted based on the needs of the learners. As the intervention level or need increases in intensity, the frequency of progress monitoring should increase as well.

Progress monitoring may be used at all three levels of the RtI model. As a compliment to high-quality instruction and universal screening in Tier 1, progress monitoring through curriculum-based measurement may be used to assess the progress of students over time (Mellard & Johnson, 2008). Teachers can use the information from progress monitoring to determine if instruction is meeting the needs of the entire class. These data can be used to judge the rate of growth for the class as well as determine the overall effectiveness of instruction. If the majority of the class fails to achieve at the growth rate necessary for meeting year-end progress goals, then the teacher may need to evaluate instructional procedures and make changes to accelerate student growth (McDougal et al., 2010). Administrators may also use these data as an indicator of areas of weakness that require additional support from instructional specialists and to determine the appropriate professional development for teachers. Progress monitoring also offers teachers a method to evaluate the quality of the differentiated instruction offered to gifted students as a part of high-quality, research-based regular classroom instruction. For gifted students, progress monitoring along with dynamic assessments and other assessments that measure complex products and performances can provide evidence for future curricular adjustments. These curricular adjustments might include acceleration, curriculum compacting, small-group instruction, or restructuring the content around concepts or problems (Rollins, Mursky, & Johnsen, 2011).

Alternately, progress monitoring in Tier 1 can identify students who are achieving at levels lower than expected and the data can be used to formulate an intervention. Predetermined scores and rates of progress should be used to determine which students need instruction beyond what is offered in the regular curriculum. It has been estimated that approximately 20% of learners will need this type of intervention, and because the intensity of instruction will be increased, this group of students will also need to have more frequent progress monitoring (Mellard & Johnson, 2008). Before referring students to a higher instructional tier, the classroom teacher should complete a controlled instructional trial and track student progress during this period of instruction

(VanDerHeyden & Burns, 2010). Students who show a lack of progress during the controlled instructional trial or accelerated progress should be considered for a higher tier of intervention, such as Tier 2.

Types of progress monitoring assessments. Four popular assessments used to progress monitor are curriculum-based measurements, classroom assessments, adaptive assessments, and large-scale assessments.

Curriculum-based measurements. Curriculum-based measurements (CBMs) generally assess basic skills needed for more complex learning (VanDerHeyden & Burns, 2010). CBMs have both elements of a teacher-made assessment and a standardized, norm-referenced assessment. Because CBMs are short (completed in 5 minutes or less), they can be as customized as any teacher-made assessment; however, the procedures, like administration, scoring, and interpretations, are standardized (McDougal et al., 2010). Examples of CBMs include sight word lists for early reading, letter writing fluency assessments, and math fact assessments. CBMs are the most popular form of assessment used for progress monitoring because they are short, repeatable, easily administered, and easily scored. The results of CBMs may be tracked to indicate student growth over time. Because CBMs measure basic skills, a teacher can analyze the errors made by a particular student and use this information to design the reteaching of the skill (McDougal et al., 2010). For academically able students, CBMs might address basic skill content that is above grade level (e.g., division in first grade).

Classroom assessments. Classroom assessments often include teacher-made assessments such as tests, products, and performances. These forms of assessment have received much criticism for their lack of validity and reliability. When teacher-made assessments address the content goals found in the instructional objectives, then the assessments may accurately reflect a student's progress (Miller et al., 2009). Another method that may increase the reliability and validity of teacher-made assessments involves working backwards from the year-end goals of a course or series of courses. By determining what a student needs to know at the end of course or, in the case of high-ability students, at the end of a course series, the teacher can design assessments that measure progress toward the goal at specific intervals. For example, if a student should be able to answer 100 multiplication facts within one minute at the end of the year, the teacher could divide 100 by the number of weeks of instruction. If a year included 30 weeks of instruction, then a student making average progress should attain approximately three multiplication facts each week. Students achieving more or less than three facts each week may be in need of an intervention. In the case of an academically able student who is attaining more than three multiplication facts each week, the year-end goal might be changed so that the student is able to move to the next mathematical operation.

Adaptive assessments. Adaptive assessments adjust according to the student's pattern of responses. As a student responds correctly, the assessment becomes more difficult, but as the student responds incorrectly, the level of difficulty is lowered (Walvoord, 2004). Many adaptive assessments are computer based and allow easy, efficient tracking of student progress. However, publishers determine the content of many adaptive assessments, and this creates a limitation for tracking progress on a specific instructional need.

Large-scale assessments. Large-scale assessments may be used to progress monitor. Because many schools use a large-scale assessment on a yearly basis, the data may be used to track longitudinal progress, but the connection between a yearly assessment and classroom instruction is typically minimal (Mellard & Johnsen, 2008). Although the data from these assessments can show specific content deficiencies, using the data to show patterns of strengths may be more challenging. Large-scale assessments are often criterion-referenced and, as such, have ceiling limitations. This creates a measurement problem for gifted students because these types of assessments do not allow for measurement of growth beyond the ceiling.

Qualities of a progress monitoring assessment. All assessments used for progress monitoring should have certain psychometric properties. Without these properties, the results have little meaning and may not be useful for designing effective interventions. It is essential to have information regarding reliability and validity on assessments used for progress monitoring.

Reliability. As discussed in the section on universal screening, reliability refers to the consistency of results obtained from an assessment. If the reliability of an assessment is low, then the scores between administrations will differ greatly, but these differences may not be reflective of student learning (Miller et al., 2009). For example, if a student scored 90% on an assessment in Week 1 and 70% on the same assessment in Week 2, the results may indicate that the assessment is not reliable. This could be verified by readministering the assessment and looking for a pattern of missed items. Repeat administration of an assessment allows the calculation of test-retest reliability, which refers to the consistency of results from one administration to the next. Administrations that occur more frequently will result in greater test-retest reliability (Miller et al., 2009). If an assessment is used for progress monitoring, it should have a high test-retest reliability coefficient for short intervals. If there is high test-retest reliability of a progress monitoring assessment, teachers can make more inferences from the results and feel confident that even small changes in a student's performance actually reflect learning as opposed to reliability issues with the instrument.

Internal consistency is another form of reliability. Internal consistency is measured through statistical analysis and should be available on most published assessments used for progress monitoring. Cronbach's alpha values greater than .80 are generally acceptable for progress monitoring assessments. Internal consistency refers to the degree of relatedness among all of the items on the assessment, and higher values indicate that the items are all measuring the same skill or construct (Miller et al., 2009). This is essential for progress monitoring because the assessment will be used to make adjustments to curricular interventions. If the assessment is measuring many different constructs or skills, it will be more difficult to create a responsive intervention using the data.

If an assessment used for progress monitoring does not lend itself to traditional psychometrics, such as rubrics for products and performances, and is scored by multiple scorers, then interrater reliability is an important concern. Interrater reliability refers to the degree of similarity in two raters' scores for the same assessment (Miller et al., 2009). The degree of similarity can be determined through statistical analysis or it can be represented as a simple percentage of agreement. When different teachers progress monitor using identical assessments, then establishing interrater reliability becomes essential. Unreliable scoring due to low interrater reliability may lead to less effective and efficient interventions because the data gained from the assessments may not be an accurate reflection of the students' needs.

Validity. Validity of an assessment refers to the interpretation and uses of the results. Construct validity is one of the most important considerations for progress monitoring because it refers to the extent that an assessment measures a construct (Miller et al., 2009). Without construct validity, the results of an assessment cannot be used as an evaluation of the presence or absence of the construct. One way to establish construct validity is to compare performance on one assessment with performance on another that measures the same construct. The correlation between the two scores shows how much the two assessments have in common, or how much of the same construct the two assessments are measuring (Miller et al., 2009). Correlations greater than .70 between the progress monitoring assessment and another assessment measuring the same construct are acceptable and indicate that the progress monitoring assessment is measuring the area of interest.

Uses of data from progress monitoring. When using progress monitoring, it is very important to score assessments and use the data quickly. The data are to be used to modify interventions based on the needs of the students, but in order to do this, the data must be analyzed. Displaying the data in a graph may help a teacher spot trends in student performance. Combining the results from multiple progress monitoring assessments may be difficult, but this approach leads to a more realistic measurement of progress. Decision rules should be created in advance of the progress monitoring (VanDerHeyden & Burns, 2010).

Most decision rules for progress monitoring rely on an analysis of trend. Evaluating an analysis of trend helps establish a pattern of change over time. The pattern can be seen visually on a graph if the growth is large or it can be calculated by figuring the slope of the growth line (McDougal et al., 2010). Visual analysis usually follows the "four-point data" rule where decisions are based on the last four data points (McDougal et al., 2010). If the last four points are above the expected goal line, then a gifted student may require a more intensive intervention; however, if the last four points are below the goal line, then the gifted student may need a less intensive intervention or may need to return to the general education curriculum. When the four points are neither below nor above the goal line, then the student is achieving as expected and should continue in the current intervention.

When the four-point data rule is ineffective, the slope of growth can be used to determine progress. To calculate the slope of the growth line, subtract the first progress monitoring score from the last score and divide this number by the number of weeks between the two scores (McDougal et al., 2010).

The slope of the line should be compared to the slope of the goal line or the expected rate of growth. Expected rates of growth may be taken from national norms or may be calculated from previous testing samples. If the norms used to figure the goal line are not on the same interval as the current progress monitoring data, then a calculation must be made to render the numbers comparable. For example, if the norms are figured on the average number of sight words gained per month, but the current progress monitoring data was collected weekly, then it would be easy to convert the current data into a monthly score so comparisons can be made. To calculate a student's rate of progress, divide the slope of the goal line by the slope of the growth line (McDougal et al., 2010). Values close to zero are a sign that the student is achieving as expected in the current intervention. If the rate of progress is less than one, the student is progressing faster than expected according to national norms and may require a more challenging level of intervention. Progress rates greater than one indicate that the intervention may not be appropriate for the student, and the situation should be further evaluated.

Diagnostic assessment. When progress monitoring does not meet the needs of a student, a diagnostic assessment can provide more in-depth information and may be used in an evaluation for special education or gifted education programs (Miller et al., 2009). Diagnostic assessments are used to design interventions based on individual needs and should reveal a pattern of strengths and weakness. When progress monitoring continues to show a discrepancy between expected growth and student achievement, a diagnostic assessment may provide the information necessary to identify specific strengths and weakness that need to be addressed by a specialist. Before a diagnostic assessment is scheduled, the multidisciplinary team responsible for instructional decisions for the student should meet and review existing data (McDougal et al., 2010). It may not be necessary to conduct a comprehensive evaluation if the existing data supports the need for individualized interventions; however, if the review of existing data reveals a need for additional information, this need can be met by a diagnostic assessment.

A trained specialist, such as a school psychologist or clinician, administers the diagnostic assessment to an individual student (Miller et al., 2009). As a part of a comprehensive evaluation, diagnostic assessments target a specific academic or behavioral need, such as needs in math identified through the Screening Assessment for Gifted Elementary and Middle School Students (SAGES-2; Johnsen & Corn, 2001) or KeyMath3 Diagnostic Assessment (Connolly, 2007). Diagnostic assessments are typically more expensive and time consuming than measures of progress monitoring and, as such, should be administered with the lowest frequency of all assessments in RtI. The information gained from a diagnostic assessment may be used to design an individualized instructional intervention or to select specific curriculum to meet an individual student's need.

Types of diagnostic assessments. Diagnostic assessments are used to examine specific strengths and weaknesses of students. They may be teacher-made or norm-referenced, standardized achievement and aptitude tests.

Teacher-made diagnostic assessments. Teachers can create diagnostic assessments to analyze common learning errors (McDougal et al., 2010). These assessments are typically used during instruction and contain a limited sample of items related to a specific type of error. In math, a teacher-made diagnostic assessment for two-digit multiplication may contain problems to test for mistakes related to place value. By examining a sample of two-digit multiplication problems, the teacher can look for specific errors related to the place value in the two partial products. If mistakes are found in student work, the teacher can reteach the concept. The goal of these assessments is to find persistent errors and provide diagnostic teaching (Riccomini & Witzel, 2010).

Teachers may also make modifications to the learning process, which are sometimes described as dynamic assessments. These focus on the interaction between the student and the task, with the teacher providing assistance as needed (Swanson & Lussier, 2001). If the dynamic assessment is designed to examine abilities and discover above-grade-level or more complex performances, then the assessment must be novel, problem-based, and require complex strategies (Geary & Brown, 1991;

Scruggs & Mastropieri, 1985). On the other hand, if the assessment is used to identify whether or not the student is able to learn grade-level content, then the teacher might modify the format, use more examples, provide information on successful strategies, or offer more direct hints or prompts (Bransford, Delclos, Vye, Burns, & Hasselbring, 1987).

Teachers might also need to use products and/or performance data to assess content, product, and process and the student's understanding of more sophisticated, complex concepts and principles in more authentic contexts (Renzulli & Callahan, 2008; Wiggins, 1993). Product assessments may include essays, books, charts, posters, DVDs, and the like, whereas performances may include oral discussions, debates, presentations, and role-plays, among others. VanTassel-Baska (2008) has identified five criteria in the design of these assessments: an emphasis on thinking and problem solving, off-level tasks that are challenging, open-ended formats to encourage creative responses, use of manipulatives for solving difficult problems, and opportunities for self-reflection. Performance assessments and product assessments may be used together.

All of these different forms of diagnostic assessments may be kept in a portfolio. The portfolio would then provide a sample of students' strengths and weaknesses, their progress, and their accomplishments (Arter & McTighe, 2001). If the student is showing work in a professional field, a committee that shares well-trained perspectives might be involved in reviewing the portfolio (Royer, Cisero, & Carlo, 1993).

Achievement tests. Achievement test batteries can provide an overall measure of student performance in different areas of the curriculum and may also be predictive of future performance in some academic areas (Miller et al., 2009). Many publishers create survey batteries that can be compared across subjects. These batteries use a criterion-referenced interpretation to provide information on student strengths and weaknesses in different subjects and may also provide diagnostic information useful for instructional decisions (McDougal et al., 2010). The Metropolitan Achievement Tests (Harcourt Educational Measurement, 2001), the Stanford Achievement Test (Harcourt Assessment, 2003), the California Achievement Tests (CTB Macmillan/McGraw-Hill, 1993), and the TerraNova (CTB Macmillan/McGraw-Hill, 2009) all contain survey and diagnostic assessment batteries that can be used for instructional and diagnostic purposes (Miller et al., 2009). To address ceiling effects, schools should use achievement batteries that are above grade level or cover multiple grade levels such as the Test of Mathematical Abilities for Gifted Students (TOMAGS; Ryser & Johnsen, 1998).

Aptitude tests. Aptitude tests are considered predictive of some type of future performance. Aptitude and achievement tests share similar predictive power toward related academic areas, but aptitude tests can also be used in situations where achievement tests would not be effective, such as in situations where a student has had little to no instruction in a particular subject (Miller et al., 2009). Aptitude tests that measure general problem-solving, verbal, and numerical abilities or abstract reasoning measure constructs that are not necessarily related to school experience. Scores from these types of aptitude tests may not necessarily correlate well with subject-based achievement test scores, especially for students who may be underachievers; however, school-oriented aptitude test scores may correlate highly with subject-based achievement test scores for these students, because the school-oriented aptitude tests are measuring constructs related to school performance (Walvoord, 2004).

A common misconception is to consider aptitude scores as a measure of intelligence, but this is a misinterpretation of the measurement. The constructs measured by these assessments describe abilities that are useful in learning, but these constructs should not be viewed as innate or fixed capacities (Gottfredson, 2003). Scores on aptitude tests can fluctuate due to a number of factors, including emotional states, attention levels, boredom, and even recent school experiences. The results from these assessments are best viewed as indicators of a student's present academic performance.

Some common norm-referenced aptitude assessments have parallel achievement tests that have been normed on the same population. This allows comparisons between achievement and aptitude. Aptitude measures that are group administered, such as the Otis-Lennon School Ability Test (OLSAT; Pearson, 2003), often correspond to achievement batteries that are also group administered (Miller et al., 2009). Common group-administered ability tests and the corresponding achievement tests are listed in Table 4.

Table 4

Common Group-Administered Ability and Achievement Tests

Group Administered Ability Test	Achievement Test
Otis-Lennon School Ability Test	Stanford Achievement Series
	Metropolitan Achievement Tests
Cognitive Abilities Test	Iowa Tests of Basic Skills
	Iowa Tests of Educational Development
Tests of Cognitive Skills	California Achievement Tests
	TerraNova

Note. Adapted from Miller et al., 2009.

Group-administered aptitude assessments may not discriminate accurately among extremely high- and extremely low-achieving students (Miller et al., 2009). For these students, an individually administered test of learning abilities may be more appropriate. A psychologist or other trained professional should administer individual aptitude or intelligence tests. The fifth edition of the Stanford-Binet Intelligence Scales (Roid, 2003) measures five factors and two domains within each factor. The two domains are verbal and nonverbal, which makes this test suitable for students with disabilities and limited English proficiency. The five factors include Fluid Reasoning, Knowledge, Quantitative Reasoning, Visual-Spatial Processing, and Working Memory. Another individually administered intelligence is the Wechsler Intelligence Scale for Children (WISC-IV; Wechsler, 2003), which has versions for examinees from age 3 through adolescence (Flanagan & Kaufman, 2004). The WISC-IV is composed of 10 subtests that are to be administered in an alternating pattern between verbal and performance measures. The Differential Ability Scales-II (DAS-II; Elliott, 2007) measures verbal, nonverbal reasoning, and spatial ability through 20 subtests and is suitable for ages 2 years 6 months through 17 years 11 months. Each of these individually administered assessments has different ceilings that contribute to the discriminative ability among gifted students. Table 5 displays commonly reported ceilings associated with each assessment overall as well as the ceiling reported on the subtests. This information should be taken into consideration when using individual diagnostic assessments with students performing more than three standard deviations above the norm.

Table 5
Commonly Reported Ceilings

Test	Ceiling
Differential Abilities Scales-II	175
Stanford-Binet Intelligence Scales (5th ed.)	160
Stanford-Binet Intelligence Scales (4th ed.)	164
Stanford-Binet Intelligence Scales (Form L-M)	164
WAIS	160
WISC-IV	160 (210 with extended norms)
WPPSI-R	160
WPPSI-III	160
WISC-III	160

Note. Adapted from http://www.hoagiesgifted.org/highly_profoundly.htm.

SUMMARY

Monitoring student progress allows teachers to make instructional decisions based on data from formative assessments. Formative assessments are used to measure current knowledge as well as to track progress toward a specific goal. Results from formative assessments need to have adequate reliability, a psychometric property that allows increased confidence in the consistency of the results. In addition to reliability, the instruments used in monitoring progress should be valid for the purpose and groups assessed.

Formative assessments can be used to address instructional needs. The data collected from universal screenings can be used to make prescriptive adjustments to the core curriculum that support the academic achievement of the majority of students. Progress monitoring data may be used to validate these changes or may be used to track performance of specific groups or individual students. When progress monitoring reveals a need for additional information on a specific student, a diagnostic assessment can provide a profile of strengths and weaknesses. The profile can be used to design individualized instruction to address specific needs.

CHAPTER

5

Collaboration

· ·

lthough all of the RtI components are important, collaboration is one component that must be present when
implementing an RtI model on a campus or in a school district, especially when the focus is on serving all students.
"Perhaps the area of greatest potential to aid the classroom teacher in
the RtI model is in the area of collaboration" (Hughes & Rollins, 2009, p.
36). Both the standard protocol model and the problem-solving model
provide for collaboration between general education teachers and
special educators (Hughes et al., 2011). Collaboration is what guides
student-centered interventions. Collaboration through multi-expert
discussions enables educators to come to a consensus of measurable
outcomes for students (Pereles et al., 2011). In fact, Patterson, Syverud,
and Seabrooks-Blackmore (2008) suggested, "with the reauthorization
of Individuals with Disabilities Education Act (IDEA 2004) and No
Child Left Behind legislation (2001), the call for collaboration is omni-
present" (p. 16).

It is through collaboration that all stakeholders involved in working with students can bring their expertise to the table for discussion in order to help students be successful in all areas. Thus, RtI is a collaborative approach to serving students. It redefines the meaning of teacher collaboration and accommodation for students at all levels (Gardiner, 2006). Collaboration among experts and professionals in a school and district "communicates to students and parents that expert knowledge and skills are valued, accessed, and shared among general and special educators. Moreover, it communicates to stakeholders that the education of every student is a shared responsibility" (Patterson et al., 2008, p. 17). To implement a successful RtI process, there must be excellent collaboration among its stakeholders (Mahdavi & Beebe-Frankenberger, 2009).

When assessing an RtI model on a school campus, it is essential that it be a comprehensive model that incorporates all learners on the campus, including gifted students. Although RtI traditionally has been viewed as an alternate way to identify students with learning difficulties, it should also be used to identify students with strengths. In order to assess whether or not campus collaboration is incorporating gifted learners, the following questions should be asked:

- Are families actively involved in the collaborative planning process?
- Does the collaborative RtI team include educators in gifted education?
- Does professional development include information about advanced students?
- Are teachers trained to use evidence-based strategies in gifted education such as acceleration, content extensions, high-level problem solving, and ability grouping?
- Do administrators in your district support the inclusion of gifted or academically advanced students in the RtI model? (Rollins, Mursky, Shah-Coltrane, & Johnsen, 2009, p. 29)

One of the key assumptions of RtI is that students are receiving appropriate instruction in the general education classroom (Edl, Humphreys, & Martinez, 2009). Collaboration is an important piece in ensuring that students are receiving the most appropriate instruction.

In a procedural flowchart representing Tier III implementation, Edl et al. (2009) listed collaboration with key stakeholders as the first of five general steps needed for successful implementation. Through collaboration, ideas and strategies from different professionals can be discussed and used in the problem-solving process when making data-driven decisions about students. Data from gifted and advanced students, as well as struggling students, can be discussed. "Because teachers bring diverse knowledge, skills, and dispositions into the classroom, sharing their talents offers a means to improve student learning" (Patterson et al., 2008, p. 17). Without this sharing and collaboration between all professionals, students may not be receiving the *most* appropriate interventions and/ or services. This in turn impacts students' responses to the interventions given, especially with more and more students being served in least restrictive environments—often inclusive classrooms. "Many see collaboration as one of the hallmarks of inclusion" (Gallagher, Vail, & Monda-Amaya, 2008, p. 12), and it is this collaboration that enables inclusion to lead to student success. Without collaboration and input from all stakeholders, including educators, specialists, gifted education teachers, and administrators, there may be gaps in the services and interventions that would be most beneficial to all students.

It is imperative that collaboration occur at all levels within an RtI model early in the process so professionals who work with students are knowledgeable about how to serve these students in the best possible way. For example, when serving a student with autism, a special education teacher with expertise in autism spectrum disorders would need to collaborate with a specialist who is an expert in teaching reading. Then they both would need to collaborate with the general education teacher "who is the primary authority on the curricula and standards for a particular grade level" (Patterson et al., 2008, pp. 16–17). In the same vein, the gifted education teacher would need to collaborate with all of these colleagues if the student showed areas of giftedness. By leaving out the gifted professional in these important collaborative meetings, the child's full potential might not be met.

STAKEHOLDERS

RtI is a systemic process that involves all professionals, staff, and volunteers on a campus, within a district, and in a community. The literature discusses several important individuals in this process. An extensive list of these stakeholders, but by no means complete, includes administrators, general education teachers, special education teachers, school psychologists, reading specialists, Reading Recovery teachers, Title I teachers, interventionists, paraprofessionals, parent volunteers, parents, retired teachers, RtI coaches, instructional specialists (Edl et al., 2009; Mahdavi & Beebe-Frankenberger, 2009), teachers of English language learners (Hughes & Rollins, 2009), and gifted education teachers (Hughes et al., 2011).

Collaboration can occur at many different levels between many different stakeholders. Teachers may collaborate with other teachers, sharing strategies and ways to motivate and engage students. Specialists such as the school counselor or the school psychologist might collaborate with the general education classroom teacher in order to discuss emotional concerns or provide proactive classroom guidance. Interventionists might collaborate with classroom teachers to provide additional support for students who learn in different ways. Special education teachers might collaborate with the general education teacher and interventionists to discuss ways to accommodate or modify work according to a student's IEP or 504 plan. The gifted education teacher might collaborate with the general education teacher to discuss ways to increase higher order thinking within the classroom or with both the special education teacher and the general education teacher to educate them about and discuss best practices for twice-exceptional learners. The gifted education teacher might also collaborate with the classroom teacher and the English language learner (ELL) teacher to discuss services for gifted ELL students. The possibilities are limitless.

Strong administration leadership is crucial to successful RtI implementation. "Administrators can assist with its implementation by carefully attending to the school's infrastructure, leadership, and needed human and material resources" (Johnsen, 2011, p. 113). Edl et al. (2009) noted that collaboration between administrators and other professionals is an integral part of the process. This collaboration allows interventionists to discuss student needs in terms of curriculum additions or changes and special program needs. It also serves as a way for administrative personnel to oversee policies and follow up on necessities such as ensuring that progress monitoring data are being entered in student records on a consistent basis and that collaboration is taking place across the campus. Frequent collaboration, such as weekly or bi-weekly meetings (Edl et al., 2009), provides a consistent way to examine issues or concerns before they arise or become a bigger issue.

Collaboration between administrators across schools and communities is also a vital component of the RtI process. The experiences of others—ideas, strategies, and successes—are resources that are necessary as schools implement RtI models that will be effective in the communities in which they exist (Mahdavi & Beebe-Frankenberger, 2009).

Collaboration between school and home is another way of implementing a successful RtI model. This assures that students' needs are met by bringing additional information to the table. Information obtained through collaboration between school and home can be used for discussing appropriate intervention plans and strategies, whether it is for remediation or enrichment. Parents have a unique perspective of their child's strengths, weaknesses, and interests. They are also able to provide a school history of what has and has not worked in the past (Hughes & Rollins, 2009). Many parents don't feel that they belong in the school environment or that they are a part of the education process. Whether this is due to personal experiences parents had as students or because schools don't always readily open their doors to parents, parents need an invitation and welcome arms to feel a part of the RtI process. Collaboration is one way to cross these barriers. Various programs are another way to encourage parents to be a part of the school culture. Educational programs such as open house/meet the teacher night, fine arts night, teacher conference day, counselor information sessions, and test review night (e.g., discussing state mandated test expectations, the SAT/ACT) are examples of ways to bring parents into schools for information and conversation time with teachers and administrators. Noneducational programs such as schoolwide carnivals, teacher appreciation week, book fairs, and PTA meetings give opportunities for families to be a part of the school culture in a nonthreatening way. Building relationships between parents, students, and schools through encounters such as these is good for school success. "Sharing information to and from families raises the achievement levels and effectiveness of interventions" (Hughes & Rollins, 2009, p. 33).

Progress reports to parents are a good way to foster collaboration between the school and home. Positive phone calls, in addition to informative calls, are another vehicle for collaboration. Parents must be aware of their child's progress in order to be invested in his or her education. Edl et al. (2009) suggested sending progress notes home once a month that include details about the student's progress and information on strengths and weaknesses. This is taken from progress monitoring data and information provided by the interventionist and/or specialists who work with the student. In addition, as a way to foster the collaboration between school and home, Edl et al. proposed that the school include intervention and enrichment ideas that parents can do at home with their child. Parents of gifted students can also be involved through collaboration with policy makers and steering committees in the formulation of local gifted plans (Brown & Abernathy, 2011). Involving the parents of gifted students—as well as struggling and average students—is a win-win situation for both home and school.

WHEN RTI SHOULD BE USED

Although states continue to incorporate the RtI process, there are no universal models that give details about when to collaborate or how to do it. Many districts have jumped into making decisions as they go. Others are taking a "wait-and-see" attitude to see which models tend to be more successful. Regardless of when or how often, collaboration is a must. There are several purposes of collaboration. Progress monitoring and making data-driven decisions requires collaboration between stakeholders who are responsible for the individual success of students. Edl et al. (2009) suggested that meeting weekly is preferable to discuss students' progress and to problem solve as a committee if needed. Meeting as frequently as possible enables all involved to be sure that interventions are being implemented in a way that ensures fidelity and that concerns of all of the stakeholders are being addressed.

When it comes to discussing strategies and interventions through collaboration, the best scenario is to meet at the beginning of each semester (Edl et al., 2009). It is helpful for interventionists to meet with the general education teachers of students they will be working with. Together as a team, they can create interventions "aligned with the students' needs (based on benchmark data and teacher input) and the school's curriculum" (Edl et al., 2009, p. 227). In the same way that the interventionists meet with classroom teachers, the gifted education teacher should also meet with the general education classroom teacher. "There is great potential for gifted educators to be tapped as resources in order to better enable the general education teacher to meet the needs of potentially strong students" (Hughes & Rollins, 2009, p. 36). This collaboration can include the sharing of strategies, interventions, and questioning techniques to foster higher order thinking and problem solving in the general education classroom with all students. The gifted educator can also meet to discuss ways the classroom teacher can differentiate lessons and foster problem solving and creative thought for gifted students in the classroom. Gifted education teachers can provide direct enrichment activities to whole classrooms. In addition, gifted teachers can provide direct instruction to gifted students, those whose growth models exceed their peers, as they move up the RtI pyramid for more individualized and intensive differentiated lessons. Specific strategies might include contracts, compacting, and acceleration. For gifted students who need even more intensive differentiation, the gifted education teacher might recommend practices such as grade skipping, Advanced Placement (AP) classes, or early college classes (Hughes & Rollins, 2009). In addition, gifted education personnel can help to gather data and provide ongoing assessment for students showing possible strengths (Hughes et al., 2011).

Collaboration between regular educators and the gifted education teacher is particularly important for twice-exceptional students who have not yet been formally identified as gifted. "One of the strongest aspects of the collaborative process is the ability to meet the needs of twice-exceptional learners" (Hughes & Rollins, 2009, p. 37). Twice-exceptional students must be nurtured in their areas of strength and receive remediation in areas of weakness in order to reach their potential (Winebrenner, 2003). One of the best ways to ensure success with twice-exceptional students is by allowing them to be a part of gifted instruction (Baum & Owen, 2004). Twice-exceptional students tend to only reach the potential of their learning disability if their gifts aren't nurtured (Holliday, Koller, & Thomas, 1999). Ongoing collaboration in this process is critical. Too often, monitoring of achievement is not done often enough and there are missed opportunities for both acceleration and remediation (Pereles et al., 2011). By bringing gifted education to the collaboration table, gifted students can be offered a seamless educational approach rather than a disjointed array of services, which is the usual service delivery model for twice-exceptional students (Hughes, 2009).

By accessing the gifted teacher's expertise through collaboration with other educators, assistance with differentiating can help "counter the argument of 'I just don't have time or know how to meet everyone's needs'" (Hughes & Rollins, 2009, p. 36). Although the gifted teacher is the expert in the area of giftedness on the campus, if gifted students are included within the RtI model, all educators need professional development on this topic, including understanding gifted characteristics and learning strategies that are effective with these students (Johnsen, 2011). Having an RtI model that brings all stakeholders to the table, including those with gifted resources, brings professional value through collaboration and understanding. In turn, this provides an avenue to build professional respect for gifted education and the field itself (Hughes & Rollins, 2009).

HOW RTI SHOULD BE USED

Although the importance of collaboration is clear, it may seem impossible to add one more component to the busy day of a teacher. However, there are ways to incorporate collaboration within the framework of RtI. Mahdavi and Beebe-Frankenberger (2009) emphasized that collaboration be linked to individual goals of the school and the community. Although difficult, it is through the collaboration effort of all stakeholders that students can become truly successful.

One way of sharing information and deciding upon what is best for each student is through a set meeting time of all professionals who might be involved in the student's educational life. These meetings can occur before school, during conference time, or after school. It is important for the meetings to occur regularly and be planned. However, even though meeting times will vary from school to school, finding time to collaborate is not always easy. "This is a wrinkle that needs to be resolved at each individual school. Collaborative teaming is essential to RtI; time to collaborate effectively needs to be scheduled into the school day" (Mahdavi & Beebe-Frankenberger, 2009, p. 73).

Another way of collaborating on a more daily basis without having to meet face to face is by keeping a daily log. The interventionist or specialist can use this log to keep track of strategies and interventions that were used, how successful they were, and ideas for further teaching. The classroom teacher, in turn, can use the log to "ask questions, offer anecdotal observation on students' success, and identify particular target areas she [wants] the intervention agent to focus on during the next session" (Edl et al., 2009, p. 231). This log can be shared back and forth between professionals as a way to have a continuous discussion in making decisions of tier movement, interventions, or possible further discussions with other professionals. In addition, the log serves as a way for supervisors and administrators to consistently monitor and keep abreast of activities that are taking place within the model (Edl et al., 2009).

THE FUTURE OF COLLABORATION: PARTNERSHIPS, PRESERVICE TEACHERS, AND PROFESSIONAL DEVELOPMENT

University–School Collaboration

With the literature discussing the importance of collaboration among professionals as an important component to serving all students' needs, the future of collaboration on school campuses resides in professional development at the preservice and in-service levels. Two articles on university–school collaboration partnerships discuss how the authors increased collaboration and ensured fidelity of RtI implementation on individual campuses. Edl et al. (2009) described the application of a Tier 3 intervention collaboration between a small Midwestern school and a Midwestern university's school psychology program. The university–school collaborative program, called the Academic Well-Check Program, emphasized the relational and collaborative nature of the partnership. The model provided additional outside sources from the university to the school so that it was able to implement a successful collaborative RtI model. School psychology practicum students worked with the district to conduct universal screeners and tri-annual benchmarks, and to design and implement both Tier 2 and Tier 3 interventions. Tier 3 coordinators and advanced graduate students worked in collaboration with personnel and parents to design a model that best served students in their particular context. The authors also noted that "sustainability is increased when stakeholders in other organizations provide support" (Edl et al., 2009, p. 236). The success of this school's RtI implementation and collaboration building was nurtured and supported by the university–school collaboration that was established.

Another university–school collaboration project was the Montana RtI Pilot Project sponsored by the State of Montana's Office of Public Instruction and the faculty from the University of Montana. This project facilitated RtI implementation in four elementary schools across the state. The focus of the project was on using collaborative teamwork in order to build unique RtI systems that would be responsive to the needs and strengths of each individual school and surrounding community. The philosophy that was adopted involved several core beliefs, one with an underlying collaborative effort of school employees: "All educators must work for all children. We can no longer afford to provide services to students based only on categories such as special education or Title I" (Mahdavi & Beebe-Frankenberger, 2009, p. 64). Focusing on the social acceptance of implementing a new program, the program continually assessed the goals and focus of the RtI model to be sure that they matched the school and community vision. One way this project aimed to create social validity was through increasing collaboration among its stakeholders. The project encouraged collaboration by providing training and support for team building. In order to provide greater support to students, the project also broadened the team responsible for collaboration and making data-driven decisions (Mahdavi & Beebe-Frankenberger, 2009). The article summarized, "to work well, the RtI process certainly requires high levels of collaboration among general and special education teachers, administrators, and specialists" (Mahdavi & Beebe-Frankenberger, 2009, p. 71). In addition, "support for collaboration must extend throughout the school" (Mahdavi & Beebe-Frankenberger, 2009, p. 71).

Preservice Teachers and Professional Development

With the mandate for inclusion and the importance of collaboration in the process of meeting the needs of all students, college faculty members are encouraged to include collaboration in their courses (Gallagher et al., 2008; Patterson et al., 2008). Knowledge and skills related to collaboration lead to successful team members who are able to interact with other professionals and parents in planning programs for students with disabilities and with gifts and talents.

Because teachers are more likely to practice strategies that they have seen demonstrated, college faculty should model collaboration with all preservice teachers (Patterson et al., 2008), demonstrating practices such as planning, implementing instruction, and sharing responsibility for teaching. Journaling was another strategy found to be useful (Gallagher et al., 2008). Journaling allowed students to self-reflect on collaboration and encouraged them to use the skills in everyday practices. Gallagher et al. (2008) summarized the importance of collaborative and teaming skills:

> If we accept the premise that collaborative and teaming skills can be difficult to master and need continual nurturance, the ideal model would be one where personnel received detailed exposure to the issues in the initial certification environment and then replication and expansion of this training through regularly scheduled professional development activities. Although teachers can develop and refine their skills as they work within a team, a lack of the appropriate foundation knowledge will surely hinder collaboration and team effectiveness. (p. 17)

COLLABORATION SUCCESS
FOR ALL STUDENTS

The extent to which school personnel are successful in teamwork and collaboration determines the success of students with disabilities and with gifts and talents in the general education classroom (Gallagher et al., 2008). Collaboration is a process that takes focus, planning, and determination. It may also require further training and thinking outside the traditional box. Skills that are necessary in collaborating can be explicitly taught so that all participants have the knowledge to work together as a team. Follow-up such as "monitoring and coaching at collaborative meetings will help keep everyone on track" (Mahdavi & Beebe-Frankenberger, 2009, p. 72). With all members of the educational team working together toward the same goal, "collaboration allows for a shared ownership for student success" (Pereles et al., 2011, p. 71).

CHAPTER

6

Professional Development for Gifted Educators Involved in the RtI Process

· ·

As mentioned in Chapter 1, it is critical that educators who are involved in the RtI process have sufficient professional development, experience, and certification(s) to implement the different tiers competently and with fidelity. Professional development for gifted educators needs to be based not only on their knowledge of the RtI process but also on their competencies on national gifted education standards as outlined in the NAGC and CEC (2006) teacher preparation standards and the NAGC (2010) programming standards. These standards provide guidance in the areas of characteristics of students with gifts and talents, assessment, curriculum planning and instruction, learning environments, and programming (NAGC, 2010). The necessary knowledge and skills for educators will vary based on the RtI tier. For example, a gifted educator needs to have sufficient knowledge and skills to collaborate with the general educator in interpreting assessments, differentiating curriculum, managing the classroom environment, and making decisions about the need for more intensive interventions. At Tier 2, the gifted educator will provide both direct and indirect services. While continuing to collaborate and coteach with teachers who need support with students in Tier 1, the gifted educator will also be teaching small groups of students who are beyond the general education curriculum and guiding them in more in-depth studies. Finally, in Tier 3, the gifted educator will continue responsibilities assumed in Tier 1 and Tier 2 and also collaborate with others in developing individual learning plans for gifted students and IEPs for twice-exceptional students. These plans may include more individualized interventions such as radical acceleration, early entrance to college, and mentorships. Tier 3 activities may also involve the formal identification of gifted students. If so, then the gifted educator, along with the psychologist and school counselor, would assume a leadership role in conducting comprehensive assessments and organizing data for making identification decisions. Table 6 shows specific professional development needs for general education and gifted educators at each tier.

ROLES OF GIFTED EDUCATORS

Similar to special educators, gifted educators assume a variety of roles within a school (e.g., teacher, collaborator, consultant, coteacher). Unlike special education, no federal mandate exists that requires educators to serve gifted and talented students. Therefore, gifted students may or may not be served with specialized programming and by a teacher with specialized training. In fact, according to the *State of the States in Gifted Education* report by the National Association for Gifted Children and the Council of State Directors of Programs for the Gifted (2008–2009), only five states require teachers to receive preservice training in gifted education, and only 20 states require any kind of credential for teachers working in specialized programs for gifted and talented students. The scarcity of teachers trained in gifted education within some states creates unique challenges for including gifted students within an RtI framework. Professional development is therefore even more critical for this group.

The five roles identified in Chapter 1 by Hoover and Patton (2008) as important to special educators are important for gifted educators as

Table 6

General Gifted Educators' Needs for Professional Development

Tier	General Educator	Gifted Educator
1	• Have knowledge of characteristics of gifted and twice-exceptional students • Have knowledge of standard protocol models that meet the needs of gifted students • Differentiate and accelerate the curriculum based on preassessment information • Organize the curriculum around broad-based themes, problems, and issues • Use off-level assessments to monitor student progress • Have knowledge of enrichment and general exploratory activities • Create a positive classroom environment, managing small groups and individual activities • Implement service-learning opportunities • Interpret assessments and make recommendations for Tier 2 • Collaborate with parents and specialists as needed	• Have a thorough knowledge of general and gifted education curriculum and models, assessments, and data analysis • Collaborate with the general education teachers, special education teachers, and parents as needed to differentiate the general education curriculum
2	• Plan, implement, and evaluate more intensive interventions for students who demonstrate above-level knowledge and skills in Tier 1 • Collaborate with parents and the multidisciplinary team of specialists	• Have knowledge of specialized interventions, specialized accelerated curriculum, technological adaptations, and assessments for students who demonstrate above-level knowledge and skills in Tier 1 • Guide in-depth studies and provide small-group instruction • Collaborate with parents and multidisciplinary team of specialists • Coteach with the general education teacher as needed to provide services to above-level students and to adapt the general education curriculum

Table 6. *Continued*

Tier	General Educator	Gifted Educator
3	• Plan, implement, and evaluate more intensive interventions for students who demonstrate above-level knowledge and skills in Tier 2 and need more intensive interventions • Collaborate with parents and the multidisciplinary team of specialists	• Have knowledge of intensive, individualized interventions; radical acceleration options; outside resources; mentors; technological adaptations; and assessments • Collaborate with parents and the multidisciplinary team of specialists • Develop individual learning plans and IEPs for twice-exceptional students as needed • Provide leadership opportunities and direct services as needed • Implement formal identification procedures

well: data-driven decision maker, implementer of evidence-based interventions, provider of differentiated instruction, implementer of socioemotional and behavioral supports; and collaborator. Although many of the characteristics within each role are similar, distinct differences will be noted in this chapter. In this way, the knowledge base of gifted educators will augment those of general and special education teachers, which will contribute to the development of all children, particularly those who have gifts and talents and those who have both disabilities and gifts.

Data-Driven Decision Maker

Gifted educators need to know how to develop, use, and implement data-based systems such as curriculum-based measurements that are *off level* to monitor students' academic achievement. They need to be acquainted with universal screeners that assess knowledge and skills across grade levels and that have a sufficient ceiling to measure a high-ability student's progress. Moreover, gifted educators need to know how to design assessments that measure more complex content, processes, and products or performances. These assessments need to emphasize higher level thinking such as problem solving, challenging tasks that are off-level, open-ended formats to encourage creativity, the use of manipulatives, and opportunities for self-reflection (VanTassel-Baska, 2008). Based on qualitative and quantitative data, gifted educators then need to make decisions about the complexity of the curriculum and the instructional level of the content. If the required content is beyond the scope of the general education classroom, then educators need to make decisions about more intensive services at Tiers 2 or 3. The gifted educator would also need to assist the team in identifying twice-exceptional students whose strengths may conceal weaknesses. As students progress through the tiers, the monitoring might include assessments well beyond grade level (e.g., end-of-course exams, the SAT, AP exams) and might include entry into a formal identification process. In this case, the gifted educator would need to administer norm-referenced tests and possess appropriate training and credentials.

Implementer of Evidence-Based Interventions

Gifted educators need to be aware of evidence-based practices that might be implemented in the general education classroom and other settings. These include tiered models in gifted education such as the Schoolwide Enrichment Model (SEM; Renzulli, 1977; Renzulli & Reis, 1985), the Purdue Three-Stage Enrichment Model (Feldhusen & Kolloff, 1986), and the Levels of Service approach (LoS: Treffinger & Selby, 2009); curriculum models such as the Integrated Curriculum Model (ICM; VanTassel-Baska, 1986); acceleration models such as the Stanley Model of Talent Identification and Development (Stanley et al., 1974); process development models such as Schlichter's Talents Unlimited model (Schlichter, 1986) and the Creative Problem Solving Model (CPS; Osborn, 1963); and domain-specific interventions (see Chapter 2). Moreover, the gifted educator needs to be familiar with specific programs for implementing in-depth studies (Betts, 1985, 1986; Johnsen & Johnson, 2007) and mentorships (Grantham, 2004; Hébert & Olenchak, 2000; Moon & Callahan, 2001). This knowledge may be applied across all three tiers in supporting a strong general education core (Tier 1), supplemental instruction (Tier 2), and intensive interventions (Tier 3).

Provider of Differentiated Instruction

High-ability students who are served primarily in heterogeneous classrooms seldom receive a curriculum that is differentiated for them. They spend much of their time reviewing knowledge and practicing skills they already know (Archambault et al., 1993). In addition, textbooks often lack challenge (Chall & Conrad, 1991; Usiskin, 1987). Because of limited services for high-ability students in the general education classroom, the gifted educator needs to know differentiation strategies to create a more challenging core curriculum. Some frequently used differentiation strategies include:

- adding depth and complexity to the content (Kaplan, 2009);
- asking higher level questions (Bloom, 1956; Costa & Lowery, 1989; Paul, 1990);
- embedding creative problem solving within units of study (Treffinger & Isaksen, 2005);
- using formative assessments and curriculum compacting to accelerate the curriculum (Reis & Purcell, 1993; Stanley, 1978; VanTassel-Baska, 1989);
- forming flexible instructional groups based on preassessments (Kulik & Kulik, 1984; Rogers, 1991);
- tiering assignments (Tomlinson, 2001); and
- using learning contracts and independent studies with students who want to extend or accelerate their learning (Johnsen & Johnson, 2007).

These strategies address individual differences in content (what students learn), rate (how quickly they acquire new information), preference (how they learn), and environment (the setting in which they learn; Johnsen et al., 2002). As students progress through the RtI tiers, gifted education teachers may be involved in coteaching with the general education teacher to differentiate or offer more intensive differentiation to gifted students such as radical acceleration options and mentorships.

Implementer of Socioemotional and Behavioral Supports

Educators need to know how to create a positive learning environment that supports the development of all students' socioemotional and behavioral development (Lewis & Sugai, 1999; Sugai et al., 2000). Although these supports are similar in many ways to those provided to all children, gifted students do present some unique characteristics that need to be addressed. Some of these characteristics include perfectionism, inner locus of control or "inner will," intensity and depth of emotions, need for self-actualization, and a highly developed sense of humor (Hébert, 2011). These characteristics may have positive or negative effects on learning and on socializing with peers and adults. For example, perfectionism may be a positive characteristic if it influences a student in striving toward excellence. On the other hand, the student may never be satisfied with her work and may refrain from turning in any assignments. Special plans may also need to be developed for gifted students with disabilities who may experience difficulties with executive functioning, interpersonal skills, and emotional control (Hébert, 2011). At Tiers 1 and 2, educators need to collaborate with other educators in developing a curriculum that targets not only academic needs but also social and emotional needs. Interventions at this level might include curriculum units focusing on identity development (Tomlinson et al., 2008), guided literature study (Halsted, 2009), biographies (Hébert & Sergent, 2005), stress management (Peterson, 2008), guided viewing of films (Hébert & Hammond, 2006; Hébert & Speirs Neumeister, 2001), mentoring programs (Hébert & Olenchak, 2000), and extracurricular activities involving social action (Silverman, 1993). For those students who continue to experience difficulties, Tier 3 activities might include individual and/or small-group counseling.

Collaborator

Collaboration has been defined as "a style for direct interaction between at least two co-equal parties voluntarily engaged in shared decision making as they work toward a common goal" (Friend & Cook, 2010, p. 7). Components of collaboration include a personal commitment among the involved educators, communication skills such as asking questions and paraphrasing, interaction processes such as problem solving, programs or services such as coteaching and consultation, and context such as working with families, paraprofessionals, and other educators (Friend & Cook, 2010). All of these components require professional development.

In gifted education, consultation and collaboration approaches have evolved. For the most part, gifted specialists have provided direct service to students in resource or self-contained classrooms or provided direct service to one or more students in the general education classrooms. Although resource consultation models have been used less frequently in the field, several have been suggested. Ward and Landrum (1994) proposed a consultation model that was comprised of three levels: Level 1 involves an exploration of the issues between the gifted and general education teacher; Level 2 consists of joint planning, demonstration, or complementary teaching; and Level 3 includes a variety of professionals who are implementing a differentiated curricula. This model parallels the needs within an RtI three-tiered approach. Another approach is the Dynamic Scaffolding Model, which "builds on teachers' professionalism in order to help them extend their abilities" (Matthews & Foster, 2005, p. 225). In this model, educators participate in professional learning programs or workshops; afterward, a gifted educator follows up to help teachers apply what they have learned. Some specific areas of support that relate to the RtI process include interpreting assessment information, implementing curricular recommendations, supporting all students' strengths, and working within the school's official guidelines (Matthews & Foster, 2005). According to NAGC (2010),

> Since students with gifts and talents spend much of their time within general education classrooms, general education teachers need to receive professional development in gifted education that enables them to recognize the characteristics of giftedness in diverse populations, understand the school or district referral and identification process, and possess an array of high quality, research-based differentiation strategies that challenge students. (p. 13)

Moreover, research suggests that principals (McHatton, Boyer, Shaunessy, & Terry, 2010) and other specialists such as school psychologists (Powers, Hagans, & Busse, 2008) and counselors (Wood, Portman, Cigrand, & Colangelo, 2011) also need professional development in assuming new roles within an RtI framework and with implementing specific interventions with gifted students. The likelihood of collaboration and mutual respect is greater when all educators share a common knowledge base.

INDIVIDUALIZED AND NEEDS-BASED PROFESSIONAL DEVELOPMENT

Understanding the knowledge and skills needed for implementing successful RtI interventions is the just first step in designing successful professional development experiences. Standards for high-quality professional development have also been developed and include (a) allowing practitioners to learn in communities with other educators; (b) using adult learning principles such as live or video models of new instructional strategies, demonstrations in teachers' classrooms, and coaching; (c) applying research-based practices to instruction; (d) receiving support from school leadership; (e) providing sufficient resources for implementing the desired practices; (f) using student data and multiple sources of information to determine the effectiveness of the professional development; and (g) providing for learning differences within a change process (American Educational Research Association, 2005; National Staff Development Council, 2001).

Professional development may take many forms, including district-sponsored workshops and courses, university courses, professional conferences at the state and national levels, independent studies, book studies, mentorships with a professional in the field, online courses, online and electronic communities, Webinars, and face-to-face presentations by external consultants.

To address the professional development standards, teachers need to be involved in making choices and setting goals for their professional development (Guskey, 1999). Within an RtI framework, educators might identify the roles they need assistance in implementing, formulate goals they would like to pursue related to these roles, develop a learning plan that might involve other specialists, identify needed resources, implement their plan, document their progress, and then evaluate the effectiveness of the plan (Karnes & Shaunessy, 2004; see Figure 3). The plan in Figure 3 shows a gifted specialist in an elementary school who would like to involve himself and other educators in learning more about coteaching. As can be seen in the example, the teacher has many choices in the plan: the RtI role, form of professional development, resources, implementation steps, and evaluation. For the plan to be effective, the teacher would need to get support from the administration so that needed resources might be provided. Flexibility would also be provided to teachers' development of a plan depending upon their current instructional practices (Johnsen et al., 2002). General education teachers who are just beginning to differentiate would focus on goals different from those who are already using student data in planning and implementing curriculum. Both plans would be honored when implementing the changes required by an RtI framework. In all cases, when educators have input into the professional development, they are more likely to implement the practice.

IMPORTANCE OF ONGOING CONSULTATION AND FOLLOW THROUGH

Involving educators in planning their own professional development is not sufficient for implementing the practices in the RtI process. Follow through is essential and may involve specialists, peers, or external consultants. Researchers suggest several models: coteaching (Friend & Cook, 2010), reciprocal teaching (Wilkins & Shin, 2010), tiered supports (Myers, Simonsen, & Sugai, 2011), and coaching and other types of technical assistance from specialists (Baker & Showers, 1984; Johnsen et al., 2002). For example, with coteaching, the gifted specialist would support the classroom teacher in implementing the differentiation practice and gradually release the teaching responsibility to the classroom teacher. Observations and support might be continued even after the release to ensure fidelity. With reciprocal teaching, paired teachers provide assistance to observe one another as they implement

Individual Professional Development Plan
RtI Process

Name: _Jim Young_

School: _Woodfall Primary_

E-Mail: _Jim.Young@wf.edu_   **Phone:** _555-7056_

School Position: _Gifted Education Specialist_

Roles in the RtI Process (Check One or More for Your Focus):

_____ Data-driven decision maker

_____ Implementer of evidence-based interventions

_____ Provider of differentiated instruction

_____ Implementer of socioemotional and behavioral supports

___✓___ Collaborator

Goal(s) Related to the RtI Role:

We would like to learn more about the coteaching role.

Desired Form of Professional Development (Put a Check by Your Choices):

_____ Workshop   ___✓___ Face-to-Face With a Consultant/

_____ University Course   Coach

_____ Professional Development   _____ Online Course

        Conference   _____ Mentorship

_____ Independent Study   ___✓___ Book Study

_____ Electronic Community   _____ Webinar

Other/Comments: _Our faculty would like to do a book study followed by a coach in this area so that we may practice the skills and knowledge_

Resources Needed to Accomplish Goal (Person Responsible for Providing Resources):

Book on coteaching for group (coach)
Coach with coteaching skills (school district professional development office)
Time to meet; time to coteach (principal)

Implementation Steps:

Identify a time to meet; recruit teachers; identify coach; purchase books; have coach lead book study; practice skills in the classroom

Documentation and Evaluation:

Teachers will identify a differentiation strategy to implement in the general education classroom. The gifted specialist will coteach lessons. The coach will observe and identify the success of implementing the strategy. Engagement and achievement data will be collected on students to identify effects of the differentiation strategy.

Figure 3. Example of an individual professional development plan.

a new instructional strategy in their classrooms. This approach usually involves a planning conference, observation/data collection, and a feedback conference (Wilkins & Shin, 2010). With tiered supports, follow-up resources might be offered to teachers along a continuum to increase the likelihood that they would be successful with the practice learned during professional development (Myers et al., 2011). For example, some teachers might be able to implement a practice after observing a model whereas others might need more intensive interventions such as daily support and material resources. Finally, specialists or consultants who were involved with the initial professional development might provide classroom support and coaching on an ongoing basis to ensure that teachers have sufficient resources and skills to implement the practices in their classrooms with fidelity.

BEGINNING THE PROFESSIONAL DEVELOPMENT PROCESS

The first step in beginning a professional development program is to conduct a needs assessment. The assessment should compare the knowledge and skills required to implement successful RtI interventions with the current practices among all educators (e.g., administrators, teachers, content specialists, counselors, psychologists, exceptional needs specialists such as the gifted and special education teachers). A leadership team within each of the school buildings would then review the assessment results. This team would be comprised of individuals who have specific role responsibilities that would be important in initiating a professional development program on the RtI process (i.e., building administrator, someone with curriculum and instruction expertise, someone with a background in gifted and special education, someone with expertise in interpreting assessments, and someone who might facilitate meetings and professional development activities). In elementary schools, grade-level representation would be important; in secondary schools, content specialists and/or department chairs should be included. The team would then identify practices that need to be adapted or created. These needs would be discussed at grade-level and department meetings. Professional development plans would then be developed for the school, grade levels or departments, and/or for individual educators. The leadership team would review these plans, coordinate efforts and resources across grade levels and departments, and assist in implementing the professional development opportunities. Along with the educators who are involved in implementing the goals on their plans, the leadership team would also assist with coordinating follow-up activities and evaluating the effectiveness of the professional development.

For changes to occur in classroom practices, the leadership team needs to ensure that (a) all stakeholders are involved, (b) there is administrative support, (c) professional development simulates and models the desired practice, (d) practices are clearly described so that transfer from the professional development activities to the classroom can occur, (e) teachers have a voice in the type and degree of change that they will incorporate in their classrooms, (f) teachers receive ongoing and consistent material and human support, and (g) feedback is descriptive and nonevaluative—mistakes provide learning opportunities (Johnsen et al., 2002; Richards, Pavri, Golez, Canges, & Murphy, 2007). Even when all of these factors influencing change are addressed, challenges will occur. These may include material and human resources, communication problems, scheduling observations, teacher schedules, external pressures, other school district priorities, competing curricular programs, standardized curriculum and pacing charts, and time (Johnsen et al., 2002; Latz, Speirs Neumeister, Adams, & Pierce, 2009).

SUMMARY AND CONCLUSION

Educators who are involved in implementing RtI interventions need to have professional development to implement different tiers successfully. Due to the variation in licensure requirements and the lack of a federal mandate, professional development is particularly crucial for specialists in gifted education. Along with direct service to gifted students, gifted specialists will need to assume new roles in the RtI process. These roles will include data-driven decision maker, implementer of evidence-based interventions, provider of differentiated instruction, implementer of socioemotional and behavioral supports, and collaborator.

For professional development to be successful, it needs to be individualized. Teachers need to be involved in determining specific personal and classroom goals, in designing a professional development plan, and in evaluating the effects of the practices on their students. Ongoing support is critical in helping teachers implement their plans. This support may be delivered using a variety of models: coteaching, reciprocal teaching, tiered supports, coaching, and technical assistance. The initiation of professional development needs to be carefully crafted and involve all stakeholders. RtI requires teachers to focus on data-based decision making and a more individualized approach to serving students. These changes are transformational in nature and will require commitment, time, and energy. In the end, all students have an opportunity to benefit.

References

American Educational Research Association. (2005). Teaching teachers: Professional development to improve student achievement. *Research Points: Essential Information for Education Policy, 3*(1), 1–4.

Anderson, L. W., & Krathwohl, D. R. (Eds.). (2001). *A taxonomy for learning, teaching, and assessing: A revision of Bloom's taxonomy of educational objectives* (Abridged ed.). Boston, MA: Pearson.

Archambault, F. X., Westberg, K. L., Brown, S., Hallmark, B. W., Zhang, W., & Emmons, C. (1993). Regular classroom practices with gifted students: Findings from the classroom practices survey. *Journal for the Education of the Gifted, 16,* 103–119.

Arter, J., & McTighe, J. (2001). *Scoring rubrics in the classroom: Using performance criteria for assessing and improving student performance.* Thousand Oaks, CA: Corwin Press.

Baker, R. G., & Showers, B. (1984, April). *The effects of a coaching strategy on teachers' transfer of training to classroom practice: A six-*

month follow-up study. Paper presented at the annual meeting of the American Educational Research Association, New Orleans, LA.

Baker, J. M., & Zigmond, N. (1995). The meaning and practice of inclusion for students with learning disabilities: Themes and implications from the five cases. *The Journal of Special Education, 29,* 163–180.

Barnett, D. W., Daly, E. J., III., Jones, K. M., & Lentz, F. E., Jr. (2004). Response to Intervention: Empirically based special service decisions from single-case designs of increasing and decreasing intensity. *The Journal of Special Education, 38,* 66–79.

Bartovitch, K. G., & Mezynski, K. (1981). Fast-paced precalculus mathematics for talented junior high students: Two recent SMPY programs. *Gifted Child Quarterly, 25,* 73–80.

Baum, S. M. (1988). An enrichment program for gifted learning disabled students. *Gifted Child Quarterly, 32,* 226–230.

Baum, S. M., & Owen, S. (2004). *To be gifted and learning disabled: Strategies for helping bright students with LD, ADHD, and more.* Mansfield Center, CT: Creative Learning Press.

Benbow, C. P. (1991). Meeting the needs of gifted students through use of acceleration. In M. C. Wang, M. C. Reynolds, & J. J. Walberg (Eds.), *Handbook of special education: Research and practice* (Vol. 4, pp. 23–36). Oxford, England: Pergamon Press.

Bender, W., & Shores, C. (2007). *Response to Intervention: A practical guide for every teacher.* Arlington, VA: Council for Exceptional Children.

Berkeley, S., Bender, W. N., Peaster, L. G., & Saunders, L. (2009). Implementation of Response to Intervention: A snapshot of progress. *Journal of Learning Disabilities, 42,* 85–95.

Betts, G. T. (1985). *Autonomous Learner Model for the gifted and talented.* Greeley, CO: ALPS.

Betts, G. T. (1986). The Autonomous Learner Model for the gifted and talented. In J. S. Renzulli (Ed.), *Systems and models for developing programs for the gifted and talented* (pp. 29–56). Mansfield Center, CT: Creative Learning Press.

Bleicher, R. (1993, April). *Learning science in the workplace: Ethnographic accounts of high school students as apprentices in university research laboratories.* Paper presented at the annual meeting of the National Association for Research in Science Teaching, Atlanta, GA. Retrieved from http://www.eric.ed.gov/PDFS/ED360173.pdf

Bloom, B. S. (Ed.). (1956). *Taxonomy of educational objectives: The classification of educational goals. Handbook I: Cognitive domain.* New York, NY: McKay.

Bloom, B. S. (1985). Generalizations about talent development. In B. S. Bloom (Ed.), *Developing talent in young people* (pp. 507–549). New York, NY: Ballantine.

Bolt, S. E. (2005). Reflections on practice within the Heartland Problem-Solving Model: The perceived value of direct assessment of student needs. *The California School Psychologist, 10,* 65–79.

Bradley, R., Danielson, L., & Doolittle, J. (2007). Responsiveness to Intervention: 1997–2007. *TEACHING Exceptional Children, 39,* 8–12.

Bransford, J. C., Delclos, J. R., Vye, N. J., Burns, M., & Hasselbring, T. S. (1987). State of the art and future directions. In C. S. Lidz (Ed.), *Dynamic assessment: An interactional approach to evaluating learning potential* (pp. 479–496). New York, NY: Guilford Press.

Brown, E. F., & Abernathy, S. (2011). RtI for gifted students: Policy implications. In M. R. Coleman & S. K. Johnsen (Eds.), *RtI for gifted students* (pp. 87–102). Waco, TX: Prufrock Press.

Brownell, M. T., Sindelar, P. T., Kiely, M. T., & Danielson, L. C. (2010). Special education teacher quality and preparation: Exposing foundations, constructing a new model. *Exceptional Children, 76,* 357–377.

Bryant, D. P., Bryant, B. R., Gersten, R. M., Scammacca, N. N., Funk, C., Winter, A., . . . Pool, C. (2008). The effects of Tier 2 intervention on the mathematics performance of first-grade students who are at risk for mathematics difficulties. *Learning Disability Quarterly, 31,* 47–63.

Bulgren, J., Deshler, D. D., & Lenz, B. K. (2007). Engaging adolescents with LD in higher order thinking about history concepts using integrated content enhancement routines. *Journal of Learning Disabilities, 40,* 121–133.

Burney, V. H. (2008). Applications of social cognitive theory to gifted education. *Roeper Review, 30,* 130–139.

Burns, D. (1998). *The SEM directory of programs.* Storrs: University of Connecticut, NEAG Center for Gifted Education and Talent Development.

Burns, J. M., Collins, M. D., & Paulsell, J. C. (1991). A comparison of intellectually superior preschool accelerated readers and nonreaders: Four years later. *Gifted Child Quarterly, 35,* 118–124.

Burns, M. K., Peters, R., & Noell, G. H. (2008). Using performance feedback to enhance implementation fidelity of the problem-solving team process. *Journal of School Psychology, 46,* 537–550.

Campbell, P., Wang, A., & Algozzine, B. (2010). *55 tactics for implementing RtI in inclusive settings.* Thousand Oaks, CA: Corwin Press.

Carnine, D. W., Silbert, J., Kame'enui, E. J., & Tarver, S. G. (2004). *Direct instruction reading* (4th ed.). Upper Saddle River, NJ: Merrill-Prentice Hall.

Chall, J. S., & Conrad, S. S. (1991). *Should textbooks challenge students? The case for easier or harder textbooks.* New York, NY: Teachers College Press.

Chant, R. H., Moes, R., & Ross, M. (2009). Curriculum construction and teacher empowerment: Supporting invitational education with a creative problem solving model. *Journal of Invitational Theory and Practice, 15,* 55–67.

Chard, D. J., Clarke, B., Baker, S., Otterstedt, J., Braun, D., & Katz, R. (2005). Using measures of number sense to screen for difficulties in mathematics: Preliminary findings. *Assessment for Effective Intervention, 30*(2), 3–14.

Colangelo, N., Assouline, S. G., & Gross, M. U. M. (Eds.). (2004). *A nation deceived: How schools hold back America's brightest students* (Vol. 2). Iowa City: The University of Iowa, The Connie Belin & Jacqueline N. Blank International Center for Gifted Education and Talent Development.

Coleman, M. R., & Johnsen, S. K. (Eds.). (2011). *RtI for gifted students.* Waco, TX: Prufrock Press.

Coleman, M. R., & Shah-Coltrane, S. (2011). Remembering the importance of potential: Tiers 1 and 2. In M. R. Coleman & S. K. Johnsen (Eds.), *RtI for gifted students* (pp. 43–61). Waco, TX: Prufrock Press.

Connolly, A. J. (2007). *KeyMath3 Diagnostic Assessment manual forms A and B.* Minneapolis, MN: Pearson.

Costa, A. L., & Lowery, L. F. (1989). *Techniques for teaching thinking.* Pacific Grove, CA: Midwest Publications.

Council for Exceptional Children. (2008). *CEC's position on Response to Intervention (RTI): The unique role of special education and special educators.* Retrieved from http://www.cec.sped.org/AM/Template. cfm?Section=Response_to_Intervention&Template=/TaggedPage/ TaggedPageDisplay.cfm&TPLID=37&ContentID=8363

Council for Exceptional Children, The Association for the Gifted. (2009). *Response to intervention for gifted children.* Retrieved from http://www.cectag.org

Council of Chief State School Officers. (2010). *Common core state standards.* Retrieved from http://www.corestandards.org

Cross, T. L., & Coleman, L. J. (1992). Gifted high school students' advice to science teachers. *Gifted Child Today, 15*(5), 25–27.

Csikszentmihalyi, M. (1988). Society, culture, and person: A systems view of creativity. In R. E. Sternberg (Ed.), *The nature of creativity* (pp. 325–339). New York, NY: Cambridge University Press.

CTB Macmillan/McGraw-Hill. (1993). *California Achievement Tests* (5th ed.). Monterrey, CA: Author.

CTB Macmillan/McGraw-Hill. (2009). *TerraNova* (3rd ed.). Monterrey, CA: Author.

De La Paz, S., & Graham, S. (2002). Explicitly teaching strategies, skills, and knowledge: Writing instruction for middle school classrooms. *Journal of Educational Psychology, 94,* 687–698.

Delcourt, M. A. B. (1988). *Characteristics related to high levels of creative/productive behavior in secondary school students: A multi-case study* (Unpublished doctoral dissertation). University of Connecticut, Storrs.

Delcourt, M. A. B. (1993). Creative productivity among secondary school students: Combining energy, interest, and imagination. *Gifted Child Quarterly, 37,* 23–31.

Deno, S. L. (1985). Curriculum-based measurement: The emerging alternative. *Exceptional Children, 52,* 219–232.

Deno, S. L. (2002). Problem solving as "best practice." In A. Thomas & J. Grimes (Eds.), *Best practices in school psychology IV* (pp. 37–56). Bethesda, MD: NASP.

Deshler, D., & Ehren, B. (2009). *Content literacy continuum.* Unpublished manuscript.

Deshler, D. D., Schumaker, J. B., Lenz, B. K., Bulgren, J. A., Hock, M. F., Knight, J., & Ehren, B. J. (2001). Ensuring content-area learning by secondary students with learning disabilities. *Learning Disabilities Research and Practice, 16,* 96–108.

Dorn, S. (2010). The political dilemmas of formative assessment. *Exceptional Children, 76*, 325–337.

Dweck, C. S., & Leggett, E. L. (1988). A social-cognitive approach to motivation and personality. *Psychological Review, 95*, 256–273.

Edl, H. M., Humphreys, L. A., & Martinez, R. S. (2009). University-school collaboration for the implementation of a Tier III reading program for elementary school students. *Journal of Applied School Psychology, 25*, 221–243.

Elliott, C. (2007). *Differential Ability Scales* (2nd ed.). San Antonio, TX: The Psychological Corporation.

Emerick, L. (1988). Academic underachievement among the gifted: Students' perceptions of factors that reverse the pattern. *Gifted Child Quarterly, 36*, 140–146.

Ennis, R. H. (1985). A logical basis for measuring critical thinking skills. *Educational Leadership, 43*(2), 44–48.

Fairbanks, S., Sugai, G., Guardino, D., & Lathrop, M. (2007). Response to Intervention: Examining classroom behavior support in second grade. *Exceptional Children, 73*, 288–310.

Feldhusen, J. F., Ames, R. E., & Linden, K. W. (1973, October). The Purdue three-stage model made for a college course. *Teaching Psychology*, 5–6.

Feldhusen, J. F., & Kolloff, P. A. (1986). The Purdue Three-Stage Enrichment Model for gifted education at the elementary level. In J. S. Renzulli (Ed.), *Systems and models for developing programs for the gifted and talented* (pp. 126–152). Mansfield Center, CT: Creative Learning Press.

Feldhusen, J. F., & Sokol, L. E. (1982). Extra-school programming to meet the needs of gifted youth. *Gifted Child Quarterly, 26*(2), 51–56.

Fiorello, C. A., Hale, J. B., & Snyder, L. E. (2006). Cognitive hypothesis testing and Response to Intervention for children with reading problems. *Psychology in the Schools, 43*, 835–853.

Flack, J. D., & Feldhusen, J. F. (1983, March/April). Future studies in the curriculum framework of the Purdue three-stage model. *Gifted Child Today, 27*, 1–9.

Flanagan, D. P., & Kaufman, A. S. (2004). *Essentials of WISC-IV assessment*. Hoboken, NJ: John Wiley & Sons.

Fletcher, J. M., Francis, D. J., Shaywitz, S. E., Lyon, G. R., Foorman, B. R., Stuebing, K. K., & Shaywitz, B. A. (1998). Intelligent testing and the discrepancy model for children with learning disabilities. *Learning Disabilities Research and Practice, 13,* 186–203.

Fontana, J., Mastropieri, M. A., & Scruggs, T. E. (2007). Mnemonic strategy instruction in inclusive secondary social studies classes. *Remedial and Special Education, 28,* 345–355.

Ford, D. Y. (2003). Equity and excellence: Culturally diverse students in gifted education. In N. Colangelo & G. A. Davis (Eds.), *Handbook of gifted education* (3rd ed., pp. 506–520). Boston, MA: Allyn & Bacon.

Ford, D. Y. (2011). Don't waste trees: Standards must be culturally responsive and their implementation monitored. *Tempo, 31*(1), 35–38.

Friedman, R., & Lee, S. (1996). Differentiating instruction for high-achieving/gifted children in regular classrooms: A field test of three gifted-education models. *Journal for the Education of the Gifted, 19,* 405–436.

Friend, M., & Cook, L. (2010). *Interactions: Collaboration skills for school professionals* (6th ed.). Upper Saddle River, NJ: Pearson.

Fuchs, D., & Deshler, D. D. (2007). What we need to know about Responsiveness to Intervention (and shouldn't be afraid to ask). *Learning Disabilities Research & Practice, 22,* 129–136.

Fuchs, D., & Fuchs, L. S. (2005). Responsiveness-to-Intervention: A blueprint for practitioners, policymakers, and parents. *Teaching Exceptional Children, 38,* 57–61.

Fuchs, D., Fuchs, L. S., Mathes, P. G., & Simmons, D. C. (1997). Peer assisted learning strategies: Making classrooms more responsive to diversity. *American Educational Research Journal, 34,* 174–206.

Fuchs, D., Fuchs, L. S., & Stecker, P. M. (2010). The "blurring" of special education in a new continuum of general education placements and services. *Exceptional Children, 76,* 301–323.

Fuchs, L. S., Deno, S. L., & Mirkin, P. (1984). Effects of frequent curriculum-based measurement and evaluation on pedagogy, student achievement, and student awareness of learning. *American Educational Research Journal, 21,* 449–460.

Fuchs, L. S., Fuchs, D., Hamlett, C. L., Hope, S. K., Hollenbeck, K. N., Capizzi, A. M., . . . Brothers, R. L. (2006). Extending Responsiveness-to-Intervention to math problem-solving at third grade. *TEACHING Exceptional Children, 38*(4), 59–63.

Fuchs, L. S., Fuchs, D., & Hollenbeck, K. N. (2007). Extending Responsiveness to Intervention to mathematics at first and third grades. *Learning Disabilities Research & Practice, 22,* 13–24.

Fuchs, L. S., Fuchs, D., Powell, S. R., Seethaler, P. M., Cirino, P. T., & Fletcher, J. M. (2008). Intensive intervention for students with mathematics disabilities: Seven principles of effective practice. *Learning Disability Quarterly, 31,* 79–92.

Gallagher, P. A., Vail, C. O., & Monda-Amaya, L. (2008). Perceptions of collaboration: A content analysis of student journals. *Teacher Education and Special Education, 31,* 12–20.

Gallagher, S., Stepien, W., & Rosenthal, H. (1992). The effects of problem-based learning on problem solving. *Gifted Child Quarterly, 36,* 195–200.

Gardiner, C. (2006). Policy perspective. *Center for Evaluation & Education Policy: Indiana Institute on Disability and Community, 4,* 1–8.

Geary, D. C., & Brown, S. C. (1991). Cognitive addition: Strategy choice and speed-of-processing difference in gifted, normal, and mathematically disabled children. *Developmental Psychology, 27,* 398–406.

Good, R. H., & Kaminski, R. A. (2003). *Dynamic Indicators of Basic Early Literacy Skills.* Longmont, CO: Sopris West Educational Services.

Gottfredson, L. S. (2003). The science and politics of intelligence in gifted education. In N. Colangelo & G. A. Adams (Eds.), *Handbook of gifted education* (3rd ed., pp. 24–40). Boston, MA: Allyn & Bacon.

Grantham, T. C. (2004). Multicultural mentoring to increase Black male representation in gifted programs. *Gifted Child Quarterly, 48,* 232–245.

Greenwood, C. R., Delquadri, J., & Hall, R. V. (1989). Longitudinal effects of classwide peer tutoring. *Journal of Educational Psychology, 81,* 371–383.

Gresham, F. M. (2002). Responsiveness to Intervention: An alternative approach to the identification of learning disabilities. In R. Bradley & L. Danielson (Eds.), *Identification of learning disabilities: Research to practice* (pp. 467–519). Mahwah, NJ: Lawrence Erlbaum.

Guskey, T. R. (1999). *Evaluating professional development.* Thousand Oaks, CA: Corwin Press.

Hale, J. B., Kaufman, A., Naglieri, J. A., & Kavale, K. A. (2006). Implementation of IDEA: Integrating Response to Intervention and cognitive assessment methods. *Psychology in the Schools, 43,* 753–770.

Halsted, J. W. (2009). *Some of my best friends are books: Guiding gifted readers from preschool to high school* (3rd ed.). Scottsdale, AZ: Great Potential Press.

Harcourt Assessment. (2003). *Stanford Achievement Test* (10th ed.). San Antonio, TX: Pearson.

Harcourt Educational Measurement. (2001). *Metropolitan Achievement Tests* (8th ed.). San Antonio, TX: Pearson.

Harkow, R. (1996). *Increasing creative thinking skills in second and third grade gifted students using imagery, computers, and creative problem solving* (Unpublished master's thesis). Available from EBSCO Host ERIC database.

Hasbrouck, J. E., Woldbeck, T., Ihnot, C., & Parker, R. I. (1999). One teacher's use of curriculum-based measurement: A changed opinion. *Learning Disabilities Research and Practice, 14,* 118–126.

Hébert, T. P. (2011). *Understanding the social and emotional lives of gifted students.* Waco, TX: Prufrock Press.

Hébert, T. P., & Hammond, D. R. (2006). Guided viewing of film with gifted students: Resources for educators and counselors. *Gifted Child Today, 29*(3), 14–27.

Hébert, T. P., & Olenchak, F. R. (2000). Mentors for gifted underachieving males. Developing potential and realizing promise. *Gifted Child Quarterly, 44,* 196–207.

Hébert, T. P., & Sergent, D. (2005). Using movies to guide: Teachers and counselors collaborating to support gifted students. *Gifted Child Today, 28*(4), 14–25.

Hébert, T. P., & Speirs Neumeister, K. L. (2001). Guided viewing of film: A strategy for counseling gifted teenagers. *Journal of Secondary Gifted Education, 14,* 224–235.

Heller, K. A., Holtzman, W. H., & Messick, S. (Eds.). (1982). *Placing children in special education: A strategy for equity.* Washington, DC: National Academy Press.

Holliday, G. A., Koller, J. R., & Thomas, J. R. (1999). Post-high school outcomes of high IQ adults with learning disabilities. *Journal for the Education of the Gifted, 22,* 266–281.

Hoover, J. J. (2011). *Response to Intervention models: Curricular implications and interventions.* New York, NY: Pearson.

Hoover, J. J., & Patton, J. R. (2008). The role of special education in a multitiered instructional system. *Intervention in School and Clinic, 43*, 195–202.

Hughes, C. E. (2009). Janusian gifted: Twice-exceptional children and two worlds. In B. MacFarlane & T. Stambaugh (Eds.), *Leading change in gifted education: The festschrift of Dr. Joyce VanTassel-Baska* (pp. 183–193). Waco, TX: Prufrock Press.

Hughes, C. E., & Rollins, K. (2009). RtI for nurturing giftedness: Implications for the RtI school-based team. *Gifted Child Today, 32*(3), 31–39.

Hughes, C. E., Rollins, K., & Coleman, M. R. (2011). Response to Intervention for gifted learners. In M. R. Coleman & S. K. Johnsen (Eds.), *RtI for gifted students* (pp. 1–20). Waco, TX: Prufrock Press.

Hunt, P., Soto, G., Maier, J., & Doering, K. (2003). Collaborative teaming to support students at risk and students with severe disabilities in general education classrooms. *Exceptional Children, 69*, 315–332.

Ikeda, M. J., Tilly, D. W., Stumme, J., Volmer, L., & Allison, R. (1996). Agency-wide implementation of problem-solving consultation: Foundations, current implementation, and future directions. *School Psychology Quarterly, 11*, 228–243.

Individuals with Disabilities Education Improvement Act, Pub. Law 108-446 (December 3, 2004).

Institute of Education Science. (n.d.). *Practice guides.* Retrieved from http://ies.ed.gov/ncee/wwc/publications/practiceguides

International Reading Association, & National Council of Teachers of English. (1996). *Standards for the English language arts.* Retrieved from http://www.ncte.org/library/NCTEFiles/Resources/Books/Sample/StandardsDoc.pdf

Jenkins, J. R., & Jenkins, L. M. (1981). *Cross-age and peer tutoring: Help for children with learning problems.* Reston, VA: Council for Exceptional Children.

Johnsen, S. K. (2011). Assessing your school's RtI model in serving gifted students. In M. R. Coleman & S. K. Johnsen (Eds.), *RtI for gifted students* (pp. 103–118). Waco, TX: Prufrock Press.

Johnsen, S. K., & Corn, A. (2001). *Screening Assessment for Gifted Elementary and Middle School Students* (2nd ed.). Austin, TX: PRO-ED.

Johnsen, S. K., Haensly, P., Ryser, G., & Ford, R. (2002). Changing general education classroom practices to adapt for gifted students. *Gifted Child Quarterly, 46*, 45–63.

Johnsen, S. K., & Johnson, K. (2007). *Independent study program* (2nd ed.). Waco, TX: Prufrock Press.

Johnsen, S. K., VanTassel-Baska, J., & Robinson, A. (2008). *Using the national gifted education standards for university teacher preparation programs.* Thousand Oaks, CA: Corwin Press.

Johnson, D., Boyce, L., & VanTassel-Baska, J. (1995). Science curriculum review: Evaluating materials for high-ability learners. *Gifted Child Quarterly, 39*, 36–44.

Johnson, D. W., & Johnson, R. T. (1994). *Leading the cooperative school* (2nd ed.). Edina, MN: Interaction Book Company.

Johnson, E., Mellard, D. F., Fuchs, D., & McKnight, M. A. (2006). *Responsiveness to Intervention (RTI): How to do it.* Lawrence, KS: National Research Center.

Johnson, E. S., & Smith, L. (2008). Implementation of Response to Intervention at middle school: Challenges and potential benefits. *TEACHING Exceptional Children, 40*(3), 46–52.

Kaminski, R. A., & Good, R. H. (1998). Assessing early literacy skills in a problem-solving model: Dynamic Indicators of Basic Early Literacy Skills. In M. R. Shinn (Ed.), *Advanced applications of curriculum-based measurement* (pp. 113–142). New York, NY: Guilford Press.

Kaplan, S. N. (2009). The grid: A model to construct differentiated curriculum for the gifted. In J. S. Renzulli, E. J. Gubbins, K. S. McMillen, R. D. Eckert, & C. A. Little (Eds.), *Systems and models for developing programs for the gifted and talented* (2nd ed., pp. 235–251). Mansfield Center, CT: Creative Learning Press.

Karnes, F. A., & Shaunessy, E. (2004). The application of an individual professional development plan to gifted education. *Gifted Child Today, 27*(3), 60–62.

Kavale, K. A., & Spaulding, L. S. (2008). Is Response to Intervention good policy for specific learning disability? *Learning Disabilities Research and Practice, 23*, 168–179.

Kavale, K. A., Kauffman, J. M., Bachmeier, R. J., & LeFever, G. B. (2008). Response to Intervention: Sparing the rhetoric of self-congratulation from the reality of specific learning disability identification. *Learning Disability Quarterly, 31*, 135–150.

Kolitch, E. R., & Brody, L. (1992). Mathematics acceleration of highly talented students: An evaluation. *Gifted Child Quarterly, 36*, 78–86.

Kovaleski, J. F., Tucker, J. A., & Duffy, D. J. (1995). School reform through instructional support: The Pennsylvania Initiative (Part I). *Communiqué, 23*(8), insert.

Krajcik, J., McNeill, K. L., & Reiser, B. J. (2008). Learning-goals-driven design model: Developing curriculum materials that align with national standards and incorporate project-based pedagogy. *Science Education, 92*, 1–32.

Kulik, J. A., & Kulik, C.-L. C. (1984). Effects of accelerated instruction on students. *Review of Educational Research, 54*, 409–425.

Kulik, J. A., & Kulik, C.-L. C. (1992). Meta-analytic findings on grouping programs. *Gifted Child Quarterly, 36*, 73–77.

Latz, A. O., Speirs Neumeister, K. L., Adams, C. M., & Pierce, R. L. (2009). Peer coaching to improve classroom differentiation: Perspectives from Project CLUE. *Roeper Review, 31*, 27–39.

Lewis, T. J., & Sugai, G. (1999). Effective behavior support: A systems approach to proactive school-wide management. *Focus on Exceptional Children, 31*, 1–24.

Little, C. A., Feng, A. X., VanTassel-Baska, J., Rogers, K. B., & Avery, L. D. (2002). *Final report on social studies curriculum effectiveness study*. Williamsburg, VA: The College of William and Mary, Center for Gifted Education.

Lupkowski-Shoplik, A. E., & Assouline, S. G. (1993). Evidence of extreme mathematical precocity: Case studies of talented youths. *Roeper Review, 16*, 144–151.

Mahdavi, J. N., & Beebe-Frankenberger, M. E. (2009). Pioneering RTI systems that work: Social validity, collaboration, and context. *TEACHING Exceptional Children, 42*(2), 64–72.

Marston, D., Muyskens, P., Lau, M., & Canter, A. (2003). Problem-solving model for decision making with high-incidence disabilities: The Minneapolis experience. *Learning Disabilities Research & Practice, 18*, 187–200.

Mastropieri, M. A., & Scruggs, T. E. (2005). Feasibility and consequences of Response to Intervention: Examination of the issues and scientific evidence as a model for the identification of individuals with learning disabilities. *Journal of Learning Disabilities, 38*, 525–531.

Matthews, D. J., & Foster, J. F. (2005). A dynamic scaffolding model of teacher development: The gifted education consultant as catalyst for change. *Gifted Child Quarterly, 49,* 222–230.

McCluskey, K. W., Baker, P. A., & McCluskey, A. L. A. (2005). Creative problem solving with marginalized populations: Reclaiming lost prizes through in-the-trenches interventions. *Gifted Child Quarterly, 49,* 330–341.

McDougal, J. L., Graney, S. B., Wright, J. A., & Ardoin, S. P. (2010). *RTI in practice: A practical guide to implementing effective evidence-based interventions in your school.* Hoboken, NJ: John Wiley & Sons.

McHatton, P. A., Boyer, N. R., Shaunessy, E., & Terry, P. M. (2010). Principals' perceptions of preparation and practice in gifted and special education content: Are we doing enough? *Journal of Research on Leadership Education, 5,* 1–22.

McKenzie, R. G. (2009). Obscuring vital distinctions: The oversimplification of learning disabilities within RtI. *Learning Disability Quarterly, 32,* 203–215.

McLean, J. E., & Chisson, B. S. (1980). *Talents Unlimited program: Summary of research findings for 1979–1980.* Mobile, AL: Mobile County Public Schools.

Mellard, D. F., Byrd, S. E., Johnson, E., Tollefson, J. M., & Boesche, L. (2004). Foundations and research on identifying model Responsiveness-to-Intervention sites. *Learning Disability Quarterly, 27,* 243–256.

Mellard, D. F., & Johnson, E. (2008). *RTI: A practitioner's guide to implementing Response to Intervention.* Thousand Oaks, CA: Corwin Press.

Merriam, S. B., & Caffarella, R. S. (1999). *Learning in adulthood: A comprehensive guide* (2nd ed.). San Francisco, CA: Jossey-Bass.

Miller, M. D., Linn, R. L., & Gronlund, N. E. (2009). *Measurement and assessment in teaching* (10th ed.). Columbus, OH: Pearson.

Mills, C. J., & Durden, W. G. (2004). Cooperative learning and ability grouping: An issue of choice. In L. E. Brody (Ed.), *Grouping and acceleration practices in gifted education.* (pp. 91–104). Thousand Oaks, CA: Corwin Press.

Minneapolis Public Schools. (2001). *Problem solving model: Introduction for all staff.* Minneapolis, MN: Author.

Moar, D., & Taylor, P. C. (1995). Teacher epistemology and scientific inquiry in computerized classroom environments. *Journal of Research in Science Teaching, 32,* 839–854.

Monroe, M. (1932). *Children who cannot read.* Chicago, IL: The University of Chicago Press.

Moon, S. M., & Feldhusen, J. F. (1994). The Program for Academic and Creative Enrichment (PACE): A follow-up study ten years later. In R. F. Subotnik & K. D. Arnold (Eds.), *Beyond Terman: Contemporary longitudinal studies of giftedness and talent* (pp. 375–400). Norwood, NJ: Ablex.

Moon, T. R., & Callahan, C. (2001). Curricular modifications, family outreach, and a mentoring program: Impacts on achievement and gifted identification in high-risk primary students. *Journal for the Education of the Gifted, 24,* 305–321.

Myers, D. M., Simonsen, B., & Sugai, G. (2011). Increasing teachers' use of praise with a Response-to-Intervention approach. *Education and Treatment of Children, 34*(1), 35–59.

National Association for Gifted Children. (2006). *Research base supporting the revised teacher preparation standards.* Retrieved from http://www.nagc.org/index2.aspx?id=1862

National Association for Gifted Children. (2010). *Pre-K-grade 12 gifted education programming standards.* Retrieved from http://www.nagc.org/index.aspx?id=546

National Association for Gifted Children, & Council for Exceptional Children. (2006). *Initial knowledge and skill standards for gifted education.* Retrieved from http://www.cectag.org

National Association for Gifted Children, & Council of State Directors of Programs for the Gifted. (2008–2009). *State of the states in gifted education: National policy and practice data.* Washington, DC: Author.

National Council of Teachers of Mathematics. (2000). *Principles and standards for school mathematics.* Reston, VA: Author.

National Research Center on Learning Disabilities. (2006). *School-wide screening.* Washington, DC: U.S. Department of Education.

National Staff Development Council. (2001). *NSDC's standards for staff development.* Retrieved from http://www.learningforward.org/standards/index.cfm

Neu, T. W., Baum, S. M., & Cooper, C. R. (2004). Talent development in science: A unique tale of one student's journey. *Journal of Secondary Gifted Education, 16,* 30–36.

No Child Left Behind Act, 20 U.S.C. §6301 (2001).

Olenchak, F. R. (1991). Assessing program effects for gifted/learning disabled students. In R. Swassing & A. Robinson (Eds.), *NAGC 1991 Research Briefs* (pp. 86–89). Washington, DC: National Association for Gifted Children.

Osborn, A. E. (1963). *Applied imagination* (3rd ed.). New York, NY: Scribner's.

Parnes, S. J. (1981). *Magic of your mind.* Buffalo, NY: Creative Education Foundation.

Patterson, K. B, Syverud, S. M., & Seabrooks-Blackmore, J. (2008). A call for collaboration: Not jack of all trades. *Kappa Delta Pi Record, 45,* 16–21.

Paul, R. W. (1990). *Critical thinking: What every person needs to survive in a rapidly changing world.* Rohnert Park, CA: Center for Critical Thinking and Moral Critique.

Pearson. (2003). *Otis-Lennon School Ability Test* (8th ed.). San Antonio, TX: Author.

Pereles, D., Baldwin, L., & Omdal, S. (2011). Addressing the needs of students who are twice-exceptional. In M. R. Coleman & S. K. Johnsen (Eds.), *RtI for gifted students* (pp. 63–86). Waco, TX: Prufrock Press.

Peterson, J. S. (2008). *The essential guide to talking with gifted teens: Ready-to-use discussions about identity, stress, relationships, and more.* Minneapolis, MN: Free Spirit.

Plucker, J. A., & Stocking, V. B. (2001). Looking outside and inside: Self-concept development of gifted adolescents. *Exceptional Children, 67,* 535–548.

Powers, K., Hagans, K., & Busse, R. T. (2008). School psychologists as instructional consultants in a Response-to-Intervention model. *The California School Psychologist, 13,* 41–53.

Ravaglia, R., Suppes, P., Stillinger, C., & Alper, T. M. (1995). Computer-based mathematics and physics for gifted students. *Gifted Child Quarterly, 39,* 7–13.

Reis, S. M., Eckert, R. D., Jacobs, J., Coyne, M., Richards, S., Briggs, C. J., . . . Gubbins, E. J. (2005). *The Schoolwide Enrichment Model–Read-*

ing framework. Storrs: University of Connecticut, The National Research Center on the Gifted and Talented.

Reis, S. M., & Fogarty, E. (2006). Savoring reading, schoolwide. *Educational Leadership, 64*(2), 32–36.

Reis, S. M., McCoach, D. B., Coyne, M., Schreiber, F. J., Eckert, R. D., & Gubbins, E. J. (2007). Using planned enrichment strategies with direct instruction to improve reading fluency, comprehension, and attitude toward reading: An evidence-based study. *The Elementary School Journal, 108,* 3–24.

Reis, S. M., & Purcell, J. (1993). An analysis of content elimination and strategies used by elementary classroom teachers in the curriculum compacting process. *Journal for the Education of the Gifted, 16,* 147–170.

Reis, S. M., Westberg, K. L., Kulikowich, J. M., & Purcell, J. H. (1998). Curriculum compacting and achievement test scores: What does the research say? *Gifted Child Quarterly, 42,* 123–129.

Renzulli, J. S. (1977). *The Enrichment Triad Model: A guide for developing defensible programs for the gifted and talented.* Mansfield Center, CT: Creative Learning Press.

Renzulli, J. S. (1994). *Schools for talent development: A practical plan for total school improvement.* Mansfield Center, CT: Creative Learning Press.

Renzulli, J. S., & Callahan, C. M. (2008). Product assessment. In J. L. VanTassel-Baska (Ed.), *Alternative assessments with gifted and talented students* (pp. 259–283). Waco, TX: Prufrock Press.

Renzulli, J. S., & Reis, S. M. (1985). *The Schoolwide Enrichment Model: A comprehensive plan for educational excellence.* Mansfield Center, CT: Creative Learning Press.

Renzulli, J. S., & Reis, S. M. (1994). Research related to the Schoolwide Enrichment Triad Model. *Gifted Child Quarterly, 38,* 7–20.

Renzulli, J. S., Smith, L., & Reis, S. M. (1982). Curriculum compacting: An essential strategy for working with gifted students. *The Elementary School Journal, 82,* 185–194.

Reschly, D. R. (2005). Learning disabilities identification: Primary intervention, secondary intervention, and then what? *Journal of Learning Disabilities, 38,* 510–515.

Riccomini, P. J., & Witzel, B. S. (2010). *Response to Intervention in math.* Thousand Oaks, CA: Corwin Press.

Richards, C., Pavri, S., Golez, F., Canges, R., & Murphy, J. (2007). Response to Intervention: Building the capacity of teachers to serve students with learning difficulties. *Issues in Teacher Education, 16*(2), 55–64.

Roehrig, A. D., Dugger, S. W., Moats, L., Glover, M., & Mincey, B. (2008). When teachers work to use progress monitoring data to inform literacy instruction: Identifying potential supports and challenges. *Remedial and Special Education, 29,* 364–382. doi:10.1177/0741932507314021

Rogers, K. B. (1991). *The relationship of grouping practices to the education of the gifted and talented learner* (Research Monograph No. 9101). Storrs: University of Connecticut, The National Research Center on the Gifted and Talented.

Roid, G. (2003). *Stanford-Binet Intelligence Scales* (5th ed.). Itasca, IL: Riverside.

Rollins, K., Mursky, C. V., & Johnsen, S. K. (2011). State RtI models for gifted children. In M. R. Coleman & S. K. Johnsen (Eds.), *RtI for gifted students* (pp. 21–41). Waco, TX: Prufrock Press.

Rollins, K., Mursky, C. V., Shah-Coltrane, S., & Johnsen, S. K. (2009). RtI models for gifted students. *Gifted Child Today, 32*(3), 20–30.

Royer, J. M., Cisero, C. A., & Carlo, M. S. (1993). Techniques and procedures for assessing cognitive skills. *Review of Educational Research, 63,* 201–243.

Ryser, G., & Johnsen, S. K. (1998). *Test of Mathematical Abilities for Gifted Students.* Austin, TX: PRO-ED.

Schiever, S. W., & Maker, C. J. (2003). New directions in enrichment and acceleration. In N. Colangelo & G. A. Davis (Eds.), *Handbook of gifted education* (3rd ed., pp. 159–173). Boston, MA: Allyn & Bacon.

Schlichter, C. (1986). Talents Unlimited: Applying the multiple talent approach in mainstream and gifted programs. In J. S. Renzulli (Ed.), *Systems and models for developing programs for the gifted and talented* (pp. 352–390). Mansfield Center, CT: Creative Learning Press.

Schlichter, C., & Palmer, W. R. (Eds.). (1993). *Thinking smart: A premiere of the Talents Unlimited model.* Mansfield Center, CT: Creative Learning Press.

Scruggs, T., & Mastropieri, M. (1985). Spontaneous verbal elaborations in gifted and nongifted youths. *Journal for the Education of the Gifted, 9,* 1–10.

Selby, R. C., & Young, G. C. (2001, September). A harvest of talent. *Parenting for High Potential,* 8–11, 25.

Selby, R. C., & Young, G. C. (2003). The Levels of Service approach to talent development: Parallels with existing programs. *Gifted Child Today, 26*(4), 44–50, 65.

Silverman, L. K. (1993). A developmental model for counseling the gifted. In L. K. Silverman (Ed.), *Counseling the gifted and talented* (pp. 51–78). Denver, CO: Love.

Slavin, R. E. (1987). Ability grouping: A best-evidence synthesis. *Review of Educational Research, 57,* 293–336.

Slavin, R. E., & Madden, N. A. (2000). Research on achievement outcomes of Success for All: A summary and response to critics. *Phi Delta Kappan, 82,* 38–40, 59–66.

Stanley, J. C. (1978). SMPY's DT-PI mentor model: Diagnostic testing followed by prescriptive instruction. *Intellectually Talented Youth Bulletin, 4*(10), 7–8.

Stanley, J. C., Keating, D., & Fox, L. (1974). *Mathematical talent.* Baltimore, MD: Johns Hopkins University Press.

Stanley, J. C., & Stanley, B. K. (1986). High school biology, chemistry, or physics learned well in three weeks. *Journal of Research in Science Teaching, 23,* 237–250.

Starko, A. J. (1986). *The effects of the revolving door identification model on creative productivity and self-efficacy* (Unpublished doctoral dissertation). University of Connecticut, Storrs.

Sugai, G., Horner, R. H., Dunlap, G., Hieneman, M., Lewis, T. J., Nelson, C. M., . . . Ruef, M. (2000). Applying positive behavior support and functional assessment in schools. *Journal of Positive Behavior Interventions, 2,* 131–143.

Sugai, G., Horner, R., & Gresham, F. (2002). Behaviorally effective school environments. In M. Shinn, H. Walker, & G. Stoner (Eds.), *Interventions for academic and behavior problems II: Preventive and remedial approach* (pp. 315–350). Bethesda, MD: Bethesda School of Psychologists.

Sugai, G., Lewis-Palmer, T., & Hagan, S. (1998). Using functional assessments to develop behavior support plans. *Preventing School Failure, 43,* 6–13.

Swanson, H. L., & Lussier, C. M. (2001). A selective synthesis of the experimental literature on dynamic assessment. *Review of Educational Research, 71,* 321–363.

Tannenbaum, A. J. (2003). Nature and nurture of giftedness. In N. Colangelo & G. A. Davis (Eds.), *Handbook of gifted education* (3rd ed., pp. 45–59). Boston, MA: Allyn & Bacon.

Taylor, C. W. (1978). How many types of giftedness can your program tolerate? *Journal of Creative Behavior, 12,* 39–51.

Taylor, L. A. (1992). *The effects of the secondary Enrichment Triad Model and a career counseling component on the career development of vocational-technical school students* (Unpublished doctoral dissertation). University of Connecticut, Storrs.

Telzrow, C. F., McNamara, K., & Hollinger, C. L. (2000). Fidelity of problem-solving implementation and relationship to student performance. *School Psychology Review, 29,* 443–461.

Terry, A. W., Bohnenberger, J. E., Renzulli, J. S., Cramond, B., & Sisk, D. (2008). Vision with action: Developing sensitivity to societal concerns in gifted youth. *Roeper Review, 30,* 61–67.

Tieso, C. L. (2005). The effects of grouping practices and curricular adjustments on achievement. *Journal for the Education of the Gifted, 29,* 60–89.

Tomlinson, C. (1995). *How to differentiate instruction in mixed-ability classrooms.* Alexandria, VA: Association for Supervision and Curriculum Development.

Tomlinson, C. A. (2001). *How to differentiate instruction in mixed-ability classrooms* (2nd ed.). Alexandria, VA: Association for Supervision and Curriculum Development.

Tomlinson, C. A., Kaplan, S. N., Renzulli, J. S., Purcell, J. H., Leppien, J. H., Burns, D. E., . . . Imbeau, M. B. (2008). *The parallel curriculum: A design to develop learner potential and challenge advanced learners* (2nd ed.). Thousand Oaks, CA: Corwin Press.

Treffinger, D. (1986). Fostering effective, independent learning through individualized programming. In J. S. Renzulli (Ed.), *Systems and models for developing programs for the gifted and talented* (pp. 429–468). Mansfield Center, CT: Creative Learning Press.

Treffinger, D. J. (1981). *Blending gifted education with the total school program.* Buffalo, NY: DOK.

Treffinger, D. J., & Isaksen, S. G. (2005). Creative problem solving: The history, development, and implications for gifted education and talent development. *Gifted Child Quarterly, 49,* 342–353.

Treffinger, D. J., & Selby, E. C. (2009). Levels of Service: A contemporary approach to programming for talent development. In J. S. Renzulli, E. J. Gubbins, K. S. McMillen, R. D. Eckert, & C. A. Little (Eds.), *Systems and models for developing programs for the gifted and talented* (2nd ed., pp. 629–655). Mansfield Center, CT: Creative Learning Press.

Turnbull, A., & Turnbull, R. (2001). *Families, professionals and exceptionality: Collaborating for empowerment.* Columbus, OH: Prentice Hall.

Usiskin, Z. (1987). Why elementary algebra can, should and must be an eighth-grade course for average students. *Mathematics Teacher, 80,* 428–438.

VanDerHeyden, A. M., & Burns, M. K. (2010). Essentials of Response to Intervention. In A. S. Kaufman & N. L. Kaufman (Series Eds.), *Essentials of psychological assessment series.* Hoboken, NJ: John Wiley & Sons.

VanDerHeyden, A. M., Witt, J. C., Naquin, G., & Noell, G. (2001). The reliability and validity of curriculum-based measurement readiness probes for kindergarten students. *School Psychology, 30,* 363–382.

VanTassel-Baska, J. (1986). Effective curriculum and instruction models for talented students. *Gifted Child Quarterly, 30,* 164–169.

VanTassel-Baska, J. (1989). Appropriate curriculum for the gifted. In J. F. Feldhusen, J. VanTassel-Baska, & K. Seeley (Eds.), *Excellence in educating the gifted* (pp. 175–191). Denver, CO: Love.

VanTassel-Baska, J. (2004). Educational decision making on acceleration and grouping. In L. E. Brody (Ed.), *Grouping and acceleration practices in gifted education* (pp. 69–80). Thousand Oaks, CA: Corwin Press.

VanTassel-Baska, J. (2008). Using performance-based assessment to document authentic learning. In J. L. VanTassel-Baska (Ed.), *Alternative assessments with gifted and talented students* (pp. 285–308). Waco, TX: Prufrock Press.

VanTassel-Baska, J., Avery, L. D., Little, C. A., & Hughes, C. E. (2000). An evaluation of the implementation: The impact of the William and Mary units on schools. *Journal for the Education of the Gifted, 23*, 244–272.

VanTassel-Baska, J., Bass, G. M., Ries, R. R., Poland, D. L., & Avery, L. D. (1998). A national study of science curriculum effectiveness with high ability students. *Gifted Child Quarterly, 42*, 200–211.

VanTassel-Baska, J., & Bracken, B. (2006). *Evaluation report to the United States Department of Education Javits Program*. Williamsburg, VA: The College of William and Mary Center for Gifted Education.

VanTassel-Baska, J., & Brown, E. F. (2005). An analysis of gifted education curricular models. In F. A. Karnes & S. M. Bean (Eds.), *Methods and materials for teaching the gifted* (2nd ed., pp. 75–105). Waco, TX: Prufrock Press.

VanTassel-Baska, J., Johnson, D. T., Hughes, C. E., & Boyce, L. N. (1996). A study of the language arts curriculum effectiveness with gifted learners. *Journal for the Education of the Gifted, 19*, 461–480.

VanTassel-Baska, J., & Little, C. A. (2011). *Content-based curriculum for high ability learners* (2nd ed.). Waco, TX: Prufrock Press.

VanTassel-Baska, J., & Wood, S. (2008). Curriculum development in gifted education: A challenge to provide optimal learning experiences. In F. A. Karnes & K. R. Stephens (Eds.), *Achieving excellence: Educating the gifted and talented* (pp. 209–229). Upper Saddle River, NJ: Pearson.

VanTassel-Baska, J., Zuo, L., Avery, L. D., & Little, C. A. (2002). A curriculum study of gifted student learning in the language arts. *Gifted Child Quarterly, 46*, 30–44.

Vaughn, S., Linan-Thompson, S., & Hickman, P. (2003). Response to instruction as a means of identifying students with reading/learning disabilities. *Exceptional Children, 69*, 391–409.

Vellutino, F., Scanlon, D., & Lyon, G. R. (2000). Differentiating between difficult-to-remediate and readily remediated poor readers: More evidence against the achievement discrepancy definition of reading disability. *Journal of Learning Disabilities, 33*, 223–238.

Vygotsky, L. S. (1978). *Mind in society: The development of higher psychological processes*. Cambridge, MA: Harvard University Press.

Walvoord, B. E. (2004). *Assessment clear and simple: A practical guide for institutions, departments, and general education.* San Francisco, CA: Jossey-Bass.

Ward, S. B., & Landrum, M. S. (1994). Resource consultation: An alternative service delivery model for gifted education. *Roeper Review, 16,* 276–279.

Wechsler, D. (2003). *Wechsler Intelligence Scale for Children* (4th ed.). San Antonio, TX: Pearson.

Wiggins, G. P. (1993). *Assessing student performances: Exploring the purpose and limits of tests.* San Francisco, CA: Jossey-Bass.

Wilkins, E. A., & Shin, E.-K. (2010). Peer feedback: Who, what, when, why, & how. *Kappa Delta Pi Record, 46,* 112–117.

Winebrenner, S. (2003). Teaching strategies for twice-exceptional students. *Intervention in School and Clinic, 38,* 131–137.

Wood, S., Portman, T. A. A., Cigrand, D. L., & Colangelo, N. (2011). School counselors' perceptions and experience with acceleration as a program option for gifted and talented students. *Gifted Child Quarterly, 54,* 168–178.

Young, G. C., & Selby, E. C. (2001). Key elements of the talent development journey. *Creative Learning Today, 10*(3), 1–3.

Ysseldyke, J., Burns, M. K., Scholin, S. E., & Parker, D. C. (2010). Instructionally valid assessment within Response to Intervention. *TEACHING Exceptional Children, 42*(4), 54–61.

Zirkel, P. A., & Krohn, N. (2008). RTI after IDEA: A survey of state laws. *TEACHING Exceptional Children, 40*(3), 71–73.

APPENDIX

A

Response to Intervention for Gifted Children
The Association for the Gifted, A Division of the Council of Exceptional Children

INTRODUCTION

The Association for the Gifted, a division of the Council for Exceptional Children (CEC-TAG) recognizes the importance and the impact of the Response to Intervention (RTI) method of identifying and serving students with diverse educational needs. The position paper on RTI issued by the Council for Exceptional Children (CEC) specifically addressed the needs of children who are "twice-exceptional" indicating that these needs must be met through the provision of "access to a challenging and accelerated curriculum, while also addressing the unique needs of their disability" (CEC Position Paper on RTI, 2007, p. 2). The inclusion of students who are twice-exceptional within the RTI framework provided a starting point for addressing students who are gifted. In this paper we extend the application of RTI to include children who are gifted.

The National Association of State Directors of Special Education and the Council of Administrators of Special Education (2006) stated that RTI "challenges the assumptions that separate, often disconnected 'silos' are the best method to address the learning needs of students . . ." (p. 4). Thus, while gifted education has organized and maintained programs separate from general education, the nature of general education is shifting. The Council for Exceptional Children (2007) has noted that RTI "must be viewed as a schoolwide initiative, spanning both special education and general education" (p. 1). Gifted education must review its relationship to general education given the framework of Response to Intervention model and the changing relationships among the components of education. In addition, the National Center for Culturally Responsive Educational Systems (2005) has noted that RTI must be addressed within the context of cultural learning and that the diversity of students must be recognized through the nature and implementation of RTI.

POSITION STATEMENT

It is the position of The Association for the Gifted of the Council for Exceptional Children that the Response to Intervention model be expanded in its implementation to include the needs of gifted children. The use of the RTI framework for gifted students would support advanced learning needs of children in terms of a faster paced, more complex, greater depth and/or breadth with respect to their curriculum and instruction. It should also be noted that students who are gifted with disabilities may need more than one level of intervention and advancement in terms of curriculum and instructional strategies.

CRITICAL ELEMENTS OF RTI

There are several aspects of RTI that are critical to its development and implementation across educational spectra, including students with gifts and talents. These components include: (a) universal screening, assessments, and progress monitoring; (b) established protocols for students who need additional supports and services; (c) problem solving that includes parental involvement to determine what the student/ child needs; and (d) a tiered system of intervention, based on level of need and support.

Screening and Assessment Issues

Universal screening is a process through which *all* students and their educational performance are examined in order to ensure that all have an equal opportunity for support. It is our contention that universal screening be applied for the purpose of recognizing student strengths and abilities in an effort to provide appropriate education to students whose development is advanced. A universal screening process helps to ensure that access to high-end learning opportunities are open for all students.

Progress monitoring, a key component of RTI, is also appropriate for students who are gifted. For these students, who learn more easily and quickly in their area of strength, progress monitoring should be used to document mastery. Once mastery has been documented, students must be given opportunities to continue learning with enriched and advanced materials related to their area of strength.

Established Protocols

Established protocols are based on standard treatments that have been shown through evidence-based studies to be successful. While these protocols have been designed to promote acquisition of new knowledge and skills for most students, they also need to include curriculum and materials that are differentiated and respond to students who are ready to learn curriculum that is beyond their current grade level. Gifted students need to be able to access a flexibly paced, advanced curricula that provides depth and breadth in their area of strength.

Problem-Solving Approach

The problem-solving approach is tailored to individual student's learning needs. When children are not responding to effective curriculum, then individualized adaptations are made. While problem-solving approaches consider primarily students who are not progressing when compared with their same-age peers, they also need to address gifted students who are not progressing at above-grade levels commensurate with their abilities. These accelerated interventions allow students to increase their levels of knowledge and skills in their areas of strengths and may include advanced educational options such as continuous progress learning, curriculum compacting, advanced placement, grade or subject skipping, and postsecondary enrollment.

The standard protocol approach uses a common, standardized curriculum in Tier 1, monitors students to identify those that are not making progress as expected, provides for collaboration among special and general educators, and refers to specialized services in Tier 3 if the students do not progress as expected. While the standard protocol approach is used primarily for children who may need additional support for success to meet grade-level standards, it needs to be differentiated and used with children who are advanced or beyond grade level.

Collaboration between professionals guides both approaches. If the general education classroom curriculum does not appear to be effective, then professionals and parents work together to develop plans for student success. This collaboration is particularly important for students from diverse backgrounds and whose achievement is uneven. These professionals need to include general, special, and gifted educators who determine when individualized adaptations are needed. If the general education classroom cannot provide sufficient improvement in all students' learning then special services are considered.

Tiered Supports and Services

The current implementation models of RTI demonstrate multiple levels of intervention, with the more significant levels of intensive intervention serving the fewest numbers of students with the most intense needs. Typical models have three levels of intervention, with Tiers I and II focused on small-group interventions, increasing in intensity to the individual level of Tier III (CEC, 2007).

When considering gifted students, each tier is governed by the intensive services required for students whose achievement is greater than typical students in specific areas. RTI for gifted students differentiates the depth and breadth, pacing, and complexity of content for students within each Tier through acceleration and enrichment opportunities. Gifted students who need more intensive services beyond the general education differentiated curriculum will move into different tiers.

SYSTEMIC NEEDS

Fluidity and Flexibility

According to the Council for Exceptional Children's position paper (2007), RTI services are "flexible and fluid, based on student need." When considering the needs of gifted children, a similar level of flexibility is needed, since gifted children, and particularly twice-exceptional students, will not demonstrate high levels of achievement in all areas. A flexible system of continuous and comprehensive services allows schools to meet the needs of gifted students at varying levels of development. In this way, services are less dependent on a student's label and more dependent on a student's need.

PROFESSIONAL DEVELOPMENT

Faculty and staff need to become aware of, and capable of, progress monitoring across a wide range of developmental levels. As noted by the Council for Exceptional Children (2007), professional development includes development of essential knowledge, skills, and beliefs and attitudes. For gifted students, such knowledge, skills, and attitudes are clearly noted in the NCATE Preparation Standards established through collaboration with CEC-TAG and NAGC (Johnsen, VanTassel-Baska, & Robinson, 2008). Such training in strengths-based educational strategies is needed at all levels of education, from state to classroom levels.

Resources

There is a wealth of literature available in the fields of gifted education and special education regarding appropriate funding. Because RTI is an allowable expense through IDEA and gifted children with disabilities must be served under IDEA, it is foreseeable that many of these services can be incorporated by realigning them to meet the needs of all students. In addition, existing funds under special education and gifted education can be aligned to meet these varying needs, using the same process that focuses on growth of all students.

TWICE-EXCEPTIONAL STUDENTS AND RESPONSE TO INTERVENTION

Nowhere else is the issue of a flexible system of RTI most appropriate than with children who are gifted with disabilities. The current system of RTI allows great flexibility in services designed to support a child's area(s) of challenge. However, it is even more critically important to support a child's area(s) of strength as well. A system in which both systems coexist and flexible services can simultaneously provide support, remediation, enrichment, and acceleration can provide a cohesive, unified system of education for children with such diverse needs.

CONCLUDING COMMENTS

CEC-TAG is committed to working with general and special educators in developing RTI models that are inclusive and respond to students with gifts and talents. RTI provides a true opportunity for all students to grow and to learn something new every day.

REFERENCES

Council for Exceptional Children (2007). *CEC's position on Response to Intervention: The unique role of special education and special educators.* Retrieved from http://www.cec.sped.org/AM/Template. cfm?Section=Home&TEMPLATE=/CM/ContentDisplay. cfm&CONTENTID=9237

Johnsen, S. K, VanTassel-Baska, J., & Robinson, A. (2008). *Using the national gifted education standards for university teacher preparation programs.* Thousand Oaks, CA: Corwin Press.

National Association of State Directors of Special Education and Council of Administrators of Special Education (2006). *Response to Intervention: A joint paper by the National Association of State Directors of Special Education and the Council of Administrators of Special Education.* Retrieved from http://www.casecec.org/pdf/rti/RtI%20 An%20Administrator%27s%20Perspective%201-061.pdf

National Center for Culturally Responsive Educational Systems. (2005). *Cultural considerations and challenges in Response-to-Intervention models.* Retrieved from http://www.rti4success.org/images/stories/ pdfs/rti.pdf

NAGC POSITIONS

Approved by the Board—"the original content, research, and drafts of this position paper were developed and assembled by individuals with expertise in the area. This final version represents discussions, revisions, and conclusions of the NAGC Board to reflect the national policy position of NAGC."

ABOUT NAGC

The National Association for Gifted Children is an organization of parents, educators, other professionals, and community leaders who unite to address the unique needs of all children and youth with demonstrated gifts and talents as well as those who may be able to develop their talent potential with appropriate educational experiences. We support and develop policies and practices that encourage and respond to the diverse expressions of gifts and talents in children and youth from all cultures, racial and ethnic backgrounds, and socioeconomic groups. To this end, NAGC supports and engages in research and development, staff development, advocacy, communication, and collaboration with other organizations and agencies that strive to improve the quality of education for all students.

APPENDIX

B

Web-Based Resources for Response to Intervention

• •

Access Center

http://www.k8accesscenter.org

> The Access Center is housed at the American Institutes for Research in Washington, DC. The center's mission is to provide technical assistance that strengthens states and schools to help students with disabilities effectively learn in the general education curriculum. It provides a variety of resources related to numerous topics such as differentiated instruction, coteaching, standards and assessments, teaching and learning, and specific content areas.

AIMSweb

http://www.aimsweb.com

> This commercial site describes AIMSweb, which is a benchmark and progress monitoring system. The system contains

benchmark assessments (e.g., universal screening three times per year), strategic monitoring (e.g., monthly monitoring), and individualized progress monitoring (e.g., frequent monitoring with annual goals).

Building the Legacy: IDEA 2004
http://idea.ed.gov

> This government site provides information about Part A (ages birth to 2) and Part B (ages 3–21) of the Individuals with Disabilities Act. It is a "living" website and contains resources and information with searchable versions of IDEA and its regulations, access to cross-referenced content from other laws, the Family Education Rights and Privacy Act, video clips on selected topics such as early intervening services (RtI), topic briefs on selected regulations, and a Q & A Corner.

Busy Teacher's Café
http://www.busyteacherscafe.com

> The Busy Teacher's Café provides K–6 resources for teachers. On the site are theme-based activity pages, various teaching and classroom management strategies, printables for classroom instruction, and resources to enhance classroom instruction.

Center for Early Literacy Learning (CELL)
http://www.earlyliteracylearning.org

> The goal of CELL is to promote the adoption and use of evidence-based early literacy learning practices. The site has guides for parents, practitioners, and technical assistance providers. CELL also describes its research-to-practice developmental framework for developing its guides and tool kits, which includes domains of literacy practices and literacy experiences.

Council for Exceptional Children
http://www.cec.sped.org

Council for Exceptional Children, The Association for the Gifted
http://www.cectag.org

> The Association for the Gifted (TAG) was organized as a division of the Council for Exceptional Children in 1958. Its primary purpose is to promote the welfare and education of children and youth with gifts, talents, and/or high potential. This site includes position statements on Response to Intervention, growth models, and inclusion. Other resources included TAG's Diversity Project, TAG's newsletter The Update, ERIC Digests on gifted and talented, Pre-K–Grade 12 Gifted Education Programming Standards, Initial Knowledge and Skill Standards for Gifted and Talented Education, Journal for the Education of the Gifted articles, and other resources.

Dr. Mac's Behavior Management Site
http://www.behavioradvisor.com

> Tom McIntyre, professor of special education and coordinator of the graduate program in behavior disorders at Hunter College, provides positive strategies and interventions for promoting appropriate behavior. He includes free podcasts and videos, lesson plans, and special sections for teachers, parents, and professors of education.

Florida Assessments for Instruction in Reading (FAIR)
http://www.fcrr.org/FAIR_Search_Tool/FAIR_Search_Tool.aspx

> This site offers assessment activities in phonemic awareness, phonics, fluency, vocabulary, and comprehension and broad screeners for grades K–12. Visitors may select a category, a grade level, and specific topics, and the site will find related activities, videos, and other resources.

Hoagies' Gifted Education Page

http://www.hoagiesgifted.org

> Information about gifted and talented students' education for parents, educators, counselors, administrators, and students can be found at this site. It introduces visitors to the field of gifted education and provides other resources such as articles, books, links, conference dates, and blogs.

IDEA Partnership

http://ideapartnership.org

> The partnership reflects the collaborative work of more than 50 national organizations, technical assistance providers, and organizations and agencies at state and local levels. It provides documents related to RtI—essential elements, grounding assumptions and guiding principles, needs of the field, a glossary, and presenter guides along with PowerPoint presentations.

Intervention Central

http://www.interventioncentral.com

> Resources and products for implementing RtI can be found at this website. Tools include a CBM generator for reading, writing, and math; a behavior report card generator; and a graphmaker. Other resources include workshops, assessments, lesson plans, and worksheets in academic and behavioral areas.

The Iris Center

http://iris.peabody.vanderbilt.edu

> The IRIS Center for Training Enhancements provides free online interactive resources that translate research about the education of students with disabilities into practice. Materials such as modules, case studies, activities, information briefs, and podcasts cover a wide variety of evidence-based topics including behavior and classroom management, RTI, learning strategies, differentiation, and progress monitoring.

LD OnLine

http://www.ldonline.org/indepth/gifted

> This website provides resources related to learning disabilities and ADHD with a specific section on gifted and LD. This section includes articles, related areas, multimedia, recommended books and links, and questions and answers.

National Association for Gifted Children (NAGC)

http://www.nagc.org

> NAGC is the largest organization in gifted education with affiliates in most states. It provides information about gifted and talented students and resources such as webinars, standards in gifted education, publications, advocacy and legislation, position papers including ones on Response to Intervention and twice-exceptionality, and links to state gifted services.

National Center for Learning Disabilities (NCLD)

http://www.ncld.org

> NCLD's primary mission is to ensure that children, adolescents, and adults with learning disabilities have every opportunity to succeed in school, work, and life. The center explains learning disabilities and provides resources for parents and teachers such as effective teaching practices, monitoring progress, and universal design for learning.

National Association of School Psychologists Resources—Response to Intervention

http://www.nasponline.org/resources/rti/index.aspx

> The National Association of School Psychologists (NASP) is the primary organization for school psychologists. Its mission is to represent school psychology and support school psychologists in enhancing the learning and mental health of all children and youth. It has organized its resources by topic with a section on Response to Intervention and IDEA 2004.

National Association of State Directors of Special Education (NASDSE) Response to Intervention (RtI) Project
http://www.nasdse.org/Projects/ResponsetoInteventionRtIProject/tabid/411/Deafault.aspx

> NASDSE's members are the state directors of special education who are responsible for implementing state and federal statues and regulations. They provide information about Response to Intervention that includes policy considerations and implementation, research that validates the RtI approach, blueprints for implementing RtI at the district and school building level, and PowerPoint presentations.

National Center on Response to Intervention
http://www.Rti4success.org

> The American Institutes for Research and researchers from Vanderbilt University and the University of Kansas established this center with support from the U.S. Department of Education's Office of Special Education (OSEP). The center provides resources, tools/interventions, presentations, information about events, and a national state database.

National Dissemination Center for Children with Disabilities (NICHCY)
http://www.nichcy.org/EducateChildren/supports/Pages/default.aspx

> NICHCY is a center that provides information on disabilities, programs and services, IDEA, No Child Left Behind, and research-based information on effective practices for children with disabilities. Resources on their website include special education and disability terms in both English and Spanish and additional resources that are organized alphabetically.

National Research Center on Learning Disabilities (NRCLD)
http://www.nrcld.org

The NRCLD conducts research on the identification of learning disabilities, formulates implementation recommendations, disseminates findings, and provides technical assistance. One of its resources is a "Learning Disabilities Resource Kit: Specific Learning Disabilities Determination Procedures and Responsiveness to Intervention," which is free and downloadable. It also provides general information about RtI, PowerPoint presentations, and parent pages.

Office of Special Education Programs (OSEP) Ideas That Work
http://osepideasthatwork.org

As part of the U.S. Department of Education, OSEP develops a wide range of research-based products, publications, and resources through its partners and grantees. On its website are tool kits on Universal Design for Learning and on teaching and assessing students with disabilities.

Phonological Awareness Literacy Screening—University of Virginia
http://pals.virginia.edu

Phonological Awareness Literacy Screening (PALS) consists of three instruments, PALS-PreK, PALS-K, and PALS 1-3. PALS assessments are designed to identify students in need of additional reading instruction beyond that provided to typically developing readers. This site provides instructional videos of the PALS assessments for early literacy, ways of developing independent workstations, how to interpret PALS scores, and research.

Reading Rockets: A Critical Analysis of Eight Informal Reading Inventories
http://www.readingrockets.org/article/23373

> Reading Rockets is a national multimedia project offering information and resources on helping children learn to read. It also provides resources about twice-exceptional students and RtI. Related to RtI and universal screening, this site analyzes data from eight informal reading inventories.

Renaissance Learning Advanced Technology for Data-Driven Schools
http://www.renlearn.com

> This commercial website provides technology-based school improvement and student assessment programs for K–12 schools. Tools provide daily formative assessments and periodic progress-monitoring technology to enhance the core curriculum, support differentiated instruction, and individualize practice in reading, writing, and math.

Research Institute on Progress Monitoring
http://www.progressmonitoring.net

> The Office of Special Education Programs (OSEP) has funded this website to develop a system of progress monitoring to evaluate effects of individualized instruction on access to and progress within the general education curriculum. It provides journals, content modules on progress monitoring, searchable databases for finding CBM-related publications, and other products.

RTI Classification Tool and Resource Locator
http://www.rtictrl.org/resources

> The Center on Instruction (COI) is one of five national content centers, part of the Comprehensive Center network, that is funded by the Office of Elementary and Secondary Education and the Office of Special Education Programs at the U.S.

Department of Education. It provides resources in literacy, mathematics, science, English language learning, special education, RtI, and eLearning. Resources include research, practitioner guides, modules and training materials, tools, examples from the field, standards and assessments, and professional development events.

RTI Action Network
http://www.rtinetwork.org

The RTI Action Network is a program of the National Center for Learning Disabilities, funded by the Cisco Foundation and in partnership with national education associations. It provides resources for Pre-K through higher education and for parents and families. For schools that are getting started, it provides articles for ways of building support, developing and implementing a plan, evaluating and refining implementation, and checklists and forms. It also includes articles about RTI's essential components: tiered intervention/instruction, ongoing student assessment, and family involvement.

Scientifically Based Research
http://www.gosbr.net

This site provides field-based research in these areas: reading intervention, math intervention, writing intervention, assessment and screening, miscellaneous interventions, and progress monitoring.

What Works Clearinghouse (WWC)
http://ies.ed.gov/ncee/wwc

Established in 2002, the WWC is a source of scientific evidence for what works in education. WWC produces user-friendly practice guides addressing instructional challenges with research-based recommendations, assesses the effectiveness of interventions, implements standards for reviewing and synthesizing education research, and provides a registry of education evaluation researchers.

APPENDIX
C

State Support of Gifted Students Within RtI Models

. . . .

As many districts begin to use Response to Intervention to identify students with learning disabilities and those who are struggling in core academic areas, some are also including students with gifts and talents in their RtI models as a way to serve all students. In order to find out more about states and whether they are supporting gifted students through their RtI models, we contacted each of the states by sending an e-mail to the state gifted and talented (GT) coordinator/director to find out whether the state is incorporating gifted education in its state RtI model, and if so, how the model is structured with gifted education in mind.

Over a 4-month period in 2011, three emails were sent to each state including Washington, DC. Questions were posed and directors were invited to respond. Thirty-one of the 50 states and Washington, DC, responded (see Table C1). Within this sample:

- 10 states responded that their model does include gifted and talented students.

- 4 states responded "yes" when the support was implied or inclusive for all students.
- 4 states encouraged support of GT students through the RtI model but did not answer "yes" when asked if the model included GT.
- 18 states responded that their model does not include GT.
- 3 states responded that they are currently in the drafting stage of including GT in the state model.

Of the states that reported GT as part of the state model, Alabama, Colorado, Indiana, Montana, and Wisconsin provided the most specific information about how GT is part of the state model.

- Alabama addresses gifted education at each of the three RtI levels by using differentiation, subject acceleration, and grade acceleration.
- Colorado provides a foundation for supporting gifted education by verbalizing gifted in the state's definition of RtI; rubrics for the implementation of RtI components embed language to facilitate the instruction of gifted students.
- Indiana provides an advanced core in Tier 1.
- Montana has a PDF available entitled "Unfolding the RtI Triangle."
- Wisconsin provides a multilevel system of support leading to differentiation of the core to acceleration and mentoring.

Although the majority of the states replied that their models do not include GT, several of them did comment that their models can be adapted for gifted or used to empower gifted students even without a state model having been adopted.

Of the states that reported that GT was not part of the state model, Florida provided the most information on how to support GT. Florida explained that their three tiers differentiate for content, process and product.

Table C1
Use of Response to Intervention in the United States

State	Did the state respond?	Does the state's model include GT?	Model is in the drafting stage of including GT	How is GT part of the state's model?	How is GT supported within RtI?	Is GT part of the visual model?	Contact
Alabama	Yes	Yes			Level 1: Differentiation Level 2: Subject acceleration Level 3: Grade acceleration	No	S. Farrell N. Johnson
Alaska	No						
Arizona	No						
Arkansas	No						
California	Yes		Yes (RtI2)		RtI serves all students—addresses gifted.	No	M. Autry
Colorado	Yes	Yes		It is verbalized in the state's definition of RtI.	Identification, programming, and assessment delivered through Tiers 2 and 3. Development of strengths and targets interventions if needed.	No. The visual does not separate out any one group of students.	J. Medina
Connecticut	Yes	No					J. Hasegawa
Delaware	No						

Table C1. *Continued*

State	Did the state respond?	Does the state's model include GT?	Model is in the drafting stage of including GT	How is GT part of the state's model?	How is GT supported within RtI?	Is GT part of the visual model?	Contact
Florida	Yes	No		Each district is encouraged to add GT.	Working on gifted issues on the website—has link for RtI. The three tiers differentiate for content, process, and product.	No	D. Smith
Georgia	No						
Hawaii	Yes	No					A. Viggiano
Idaho	No						
Illinois	No						
Indiana	Yes	Yes		High ability is part of RtI.	High-ability students receive advanced core in Tier 1.	Yes. Intervention and acceleration and decision flow chart for advanced.	A. Marschand
Iowa	No						
Kansas	Yes	No		Multi-tier system empowers each student to achieve high standards.			T. Smith
Kentucky	Yes		Yes	Updating model to include GT.	Given assistance in Tiers 2 and 3.	It will be included.	G. Finkbonner

Table C1. *Continued*

State	Did the state respond?	Does the state's model include GT?	Model is in the drafting stage of including GT	How is GT part of the state's model?	How is GT supported within RtI?	Is GT part of the visual model?	Contact
Louisiana	Yes	No					M. Johnson
Maine	Yes	Yes		Serving GT is implied.	Local decisions under RtI structure—academic and behavior.	No	P. Drapeau C. Mchatten
Maryland	Yes	No		Only if they are LD.			J. Paynter
Massachusetts	No						
Michigan	No						
Minnesota	Yes	Yes		Applies to all students: average, accelerated, or struggling.			W. Behrens
Mississippi	No						
Missouri	Yes	Yes		Inclusive of all students.	Individual districts choose how to serve students.	No. Systems model, so doesn't show specific populations.	D. Welch
Montana	Yes	Yes		RtI and GT education manual.	Each district determines this.	Yes. See the model "Unfolding the RtI Triangle."	D. Poole
Nebraska	No						
Nevada	No						

Table C1. Continued

State	Did the state respond?	Does the state's model include GT?	Model is in the drafting stage of including GT	How is GT part of the state's model?	How is GT supported within RtI?	Is GT part of the visual model?	Contact
New Hampshire	Yes	No					K. Ralihan
New Jersey	No						
New Mexico	No						
New York	No						
North Carolina	Yes	Yes	Yes	Updating; available this fall.			S. Shah-Coltrane
North Dakota	Yes	Yes		Yes, but not as formally as ELL or economically disadvantaged.		No. Model is focused on tiers, not categories.	B. Oas
Ohio	Yes	No		Starting demonstration models. No state model.	Gifted services in regular classroom with interventionist providing Tiers 2 and 3.	No	E. Hahn
Oklahoma	Yes	No					S. Smith
Oregon	Yes	No					R. Blocher
Pennsylvania	Yes	No					S. Curl
Rhode Island	No						
South Carolina	Yes	No					R. Blanchard

Table C1. *Continued*

State	Did the state respond?	Does the state's model include GT?	Model is in the drafting stage of including GT	How is GT part of the state's model?	How is GT supported within RtI?	Is GT part of the visual model?	Contact
South Dakota	Yes	No		No mandate for gifted. State does not support financially.	Several districts with great programs but the state does not collect information on them.		S. Burgard
Tennessee	Yes	No (RtI can be adapted for gifted)		No mandated model but RtI can be adapted for gifted.		Plan on addressing GT in rubric.	R. Willis
Texas	No						
Utah	No						
Vermont	Yes	No		Do not have GT coordinator due to budget cuts.			N. Bryant
Virginia	Yes	Yes		RtI is an "all ed" initiative so gifted is included.	Using intervention time during the day to extend gifted.		S. Trulov

Table C1. Continued

State	Did the state respond?	Does the state's model include GT?	Model is in the drafting stage of including GT	How is GT part of the state's model?	How is GT supported within RtI?	Is GT part of the visual model?	Contact
Washington	Yes	No		GT not formally addressed; working to develop.	Local control state: Some using flexible groupings based on strengths, radical grade acceleration, and completing IB by 10th grade.	Not currently	J. Hess
Washington, DC	Yes	No					C. Colgan
West Virginia	Yes	No		No	Some GT teachers acting as interventionists and enriching content in general education classes.	No	V. Mohnacky
Wisconsin	Yes	Yes		GT is an integral part of RtI.	Multilevel system of support leads to differentiation of core to acceleration/mentoring in upper tiers.	Yes	C. Mursky
Wyoming	No						

About the Authors

. . . .

Susan K. Johnsen, Ph.D., is a professor in the Department of Educational Psychology at Baylor University in Waco, TX, where she directs the Ph.D. program and programs related to gifted and talented education. She is editor of *Gifted Child Today* and author of more than 200 books, articles, monographs, and technical reports related to gifted education. She has written three tests used in identifying gifted students: Test of Mathematical Abilities for Gifted Students (TOMAGS), Test of Nonverbal Intelligence (TONI-4), and Screening Assessment for Gifted Elementary and Middle School Students (SAGES-2). She is past president of The Association for the Gifted (TAG), Council for Exceptional Children, and past president of the Texas Association for the Gifted and Talented (TAGT).

Tracey N. Sulak, M.Ed., is a doctoral candidate in the Department of Educational Psychology at Baylor University. She has an M.Ed. in curriculum and instruction with an emphasis in gifted and talented. Her research interests are learning disabilities, assessment, and educational environments, and she has multiple publications and presentations in each of these areas. Her educational experiences include teaching in public and private educational settings as well as serving as an instructor in the special education program at Baylor University.

Karen Rollins, M.S., LPC, is a Licensed Professional Counselor in private practice, specializing in children with disabilities. She is a presenter for the Center for Learning and Development, which focuses on children with learning difficulties and ADD. She is a doctoral candidate in the Department of Educational Psychology at Baylor University. She has presented at numerous state and national conventions including CEC. Her educational experience includes teaching at the elementary and middle school levels as well as being a part-time lecturer and student teacher supervisor at Baylor University.